英語教育史
重要文献集成

[監修・解題] 江利川 春雄

■第8巻■ 英語教員講習 1

◆ ハワード・スワン講述『スワン氏英語教授法』
（*The Psychological Method of Teaching and Studying English.*）

◆ ガントレットほか講述『明治三十七年夏期金沢英語講習会筆記』
（*Résumé of Lectures Given at the Summer School of English.*）

ゆまに書房

凡　例

一、「英語教育史重要文献集成」第II期全5巻は、好評を頂いた第I期全5巻に引き続き、日本の英語教育史において欠くことのできない重要文献のうち、特に今日的な示唆に富むものを精選して復刻したものである。いずれも国立国会図書館デジタルコレクションで一般公開されておらず、復刻版もなく、所蔵する図書館も僅少で、閲覧が困難な文献である。

第6巻　英語学習法1
第7巻　英語学習法2
第8巻　英語教員講習1
第9巻　英語教員講習2
第10巻　英学史研究

一、復刻にあたっては、歴史資料的価値を尊重して原文のままとした。ただし、寸法については適宜縮小した。

一、底本の印刷状態や保存状態等の理由により、一部判読が困難な箇所がある。

一、第8巻は、英語教員講習1として、文部省主催による中等英語教員講習会の内容を詳細に伝える2つの文献を復刻した。

　①ハワード・スワン講述・安藤貫一筆記・編集（奥付では共著）『スワン氏英語教授法』（*The Psychological Method of Teaching and Studying English. By Professor Howard Swan. Arranged by K. Andō.*）国民英学会出版局、1902（明治35）年10月23日発行、四六判、全65ページ。

　②ガントレットほか講述・安藤貫一筆記・編集（奥付では安藤貫一著）『明治三十七年夏期金沢英語講習会筆記』（*Résumé of Lectures Given at the Summer School of English*（1904）*by Prof. Gauntlett, Prof. McKenzie, Prof. Elliott, Written and Arranged by K. Ando.*）三省堂、1904（明治37）年11月24日発行、四六判、全224ページ。

ともに明治期の英語教員に求められた英語力と英語教授法を知る上で歴史的な意義を有するが、現在所蔵が確認できるのは、①が1冊、②が5冊のみである。

一、本巻の復刻に当たって、資料提供を許諾いただいた各位、複写等で協力をいただいた上野舞斗氏（和歌山大学大学院生、現・関西大学大学院博士課程）に感謝申し上げる。

英語教員講習 1　目次

ハワード・スワン講述『スワン氏英語教授法』
(*The Psychological Method of Teaching and Studying English.*)

ガントレットほか講述『明治三十七年夏期金沢英語講習会筆記』
(*Résumé of Lectures Given at the Summer School of English.*)

解題　　　江利川 春雄

スワン氏英語教授法

The Psychological Method of Teaching and Studying English.

THE
PSYCHOLOGICAL METHOD

LECTURES
BY
HOWARD SWAN

ARRANGED BY
K. ANDŌ

TOKYO
KOKUMIN EIGAKUKWAI

1902

THE
PSYCHOLOGICAL METHOD

OF

TEACHING AND STUDYING

ENGLISH.

AUTHORIZED REPORTS OF THE LEC-
TURES DELIVERED AT THE TEACHERS'
SUMMER SCHOOL OPENED IN TOKYO
BY THE JAPANESE EDUCATION DEPART-
MENT IN 1902. ✒ ✒ ✒ ✒ ✒ ✒

BY

PROFESSOR HOWARD SWAN.

ARRANGED

BY

K. ANDŌ.

TŌKYŌ
KOKUMIN EIGAKUKWAI.

1902.

AUTHORISATION.

I hereby authorise Mr. K. Andō
to use the details of my lectures
to the Teachers' Summer School,
in the publication of his reports.

Howard Swan.

Tokyo Higher Commercial College.
October 1902.

PSYCHOLOGICAL METHOD OF TEACHING AND STUDYING ENGLISH.

THE FIRST LECTURE.

1st Hour.

INTRODUCTORY.

Prof. Howard Swan, the lecturer, appeared precisely at the appointed hour, half-past seven a. m., on the platform of the Lecture Hall belonging to the Higher Commercial School. Addressing the eager audience numbering 110, he said that he had been for some ten years engaged in the work of searching for some effective system of organising education. The classical system is based upon the study of ancient classical languages,—in the West, Greek and Latin, in the East, Sanscrit and Chinese. Ruskin proposed to base education upon Art, Herbert Spencer upon Science, Taine and others, upon imagination or the influence of surrounding circumstances. Language is the true basis ; and with the coming of the linguist Gouin, with his theory of sequences, it was seen that the study of modern languages might be made an efficient basis of education. The union of philology, art, science and the study of imagination, with the theory of sequences, has led to what is now termed the Psychological Method.

Prof. Swan's method of teaching English is founded on the principle of sequence or series first enunciated by Gouin, and elaborated by himself and M. Victor Bétis, of Paris.

Then followed his remarks upon the Japanese method of studying foreign languages—the method which treats a living language like a dead one, and which causes many scholars to speak it as if through the telephone. His one year's stay as an English instructor in Japan, whither he came through Baron Kanda's introduction, had induced him to formulate a special method of teaching Japanese students in the English language with success; and he expressed his desire to recommend this new method to the teachers of English. According to the psychological method, one must pay special attention to

1. The Study of Sounds ;
2. The Study of Expressions or Idioms ;
3. The Use of the Imagination, mentioning facts in sequence ;
4. The Study of the Action of Thought.

Here a psychological reference was made to the power of imagination. When we hear somebody call a *kurumaya*, he said, we picture to ourselves some man, healthy in appearance and bare-legged, holding the shafts of a *jinriki-sha*. Thus, the first principle in language study consists in associating a mental picture or an imaginary scene with sound. The second principle, is the arrangement of sentences in sequences (Lat. to follow) or series of actions.

Example :—

GOING IN A TRAIN.

1. We go to a station.
2. We go to a booking office.

3

3. We buy tickets.

4. We go on to the platform.

5. We open the door of a compartment.

6. And we get into the train.

Connections between actions must be carefully kept in order of sequence in time.

2nd Hour.
SEQUENCES OF ACTIONS.

Recommending, to begin with, Gouin's " Art of Teaching and Studying Languages," and " First Lesson" ; " Facts of Life " and " Scenes of English Life," by Swan and Bétis ; Soames' " Phonetics," and a few other books of reference, the professor entered at once into the practice of sequences of actions.

LESSON I.
I OPEN THE DOOR.

Scene: The school room ; the door.

VERBS.	COMPLETE SENTENCES.
am	I am a teacher.
is	Here is a chair.
am sitting	I am sitting on the chair.
get up	I get up from the chair.
walk	I walk to the door.
get to	I get to the door.
put out	I put out my hand.
take hold	I take hold of the handle.
turn	I turn the handle.
pull	I pull the handle.
open	I open the door.
go out	I go out of the room.

4

After personally showing the method, he made his pupils practise it, strict attention being given to the pronunciation of the words, which was afterwards indicated by a system of phonetics of his own invention.

THE FOLLOWING LESSON IS IN HIS PHONETIC SIGNS.

I am a teacher.	Aai æm ε tii-chε.
Here is a chair.	Hii-εr iz ε chè-ε.
I am sitting on the chair.	Aai æm siting oⁿn dhε chè-ε.
I get up from the chair.	Aai gét œp from dhε chè-ε.
I walk to the door.	Aai wō-k tu dhε dō-ε.
I put out my hand.	Aai put æut maai hæ : nd.
I take hold of the handle.	Aai tè : ik hold ov dhε hæ : nd'l.
I turn the handle.	Aai tε : -n dhε hæ : nd'l.
I pull the handle.	Aai pu-l dhε hæ : nd'l.
I open the door.	Aai Ⓞpεn dhε dō-ε.
I go out of the room.	Aai go aut ov dhε ruu : m.

NOTES.

1. Have two blackboards (or divide the blackboard into two parts), on one of which write out the verbs used in sequence first, and after the pupils can recite those verbs with perfection, add to the given verbs other words to make complete sentences. The other blackboard (or the other part of the board) is left for necessary notes to be copied by pupils.

2. The three pronunciations of the article " The " (Dhii:—, dhε, dhi.)

3. Distinction between " To " (movement to a certain point) and " Towards " (go round to or at a distance.)

4. Three pronunciations of "Door" (old—Duur, modern and correct—Dō-ɛr, usual dō : ɛ or dōɛ.)

3rd Hour.

READING.

The opening passage from Scott's " Ivanhoe " was first read and then the principal verbs were written on the blackboard and explained. The scene, near Sheffield, men-. tioned in 'the passage, was very familiar to the professor who had lived, as he said, for about ten years in that locality. His sonorous pronunciation and eloquent gestures were enough to produce scene pictures in the listener's brains, as the method advocates. The complete sentences were then constructed. Recitation on the part of the students followed.

THE SECOND LECTURE.

1st Hour.

THE METHOD OF TEACHING LANGUAGE.

Prof. Swan said " Good morning ! " in response to the greeting from his pupils. He then wrote on the blackboard " Good morning " in phonetics (Gu-d mō : ɛning), and made the students repeat the words all together. Explanation on phonetics was then made, in the course of which he observed that he had once thought the sounds of English vowels were 20 in number—10 long and 10 short ; that he had found 6 more later on, 3 long and 3 short, and that 3 more were now added. As an example, he discriminated 4 sounds contained in the diphthong *oo* as foot (fut), boot (buut), good (gu-d) and food (fuu-d). He remarked that almost all English dictionaries hitherto published are not authoritative in pronunciation, and even the few books on phonetics are not yet sufficiently exact. Care must therefore be taken in this branch of language study, i. e., the analysis of words and putting in signs all the particular sounds involved in them. He went on to his characteristic method of teaching foreign languages, which is no other than the one of appealing mostly to the vivid imagination of students. Since the old classical method has been found wanting, two other methods have been found practical—object teaching with pictures and the psychological method or the system of imagination. He advocates the latter for the reason that it practises the pupil to think in the language studied ; so, if properly taught, pupils can see in their mind's eye, with some help or explanation, many things which they have never actually seen or heard of, and this use of the imagination, it was insisted upon, is of primary importance in language study.

Every teacher of foreign languages should make his method as interesting as possible, so as to prevent his pupils from growing weary. It is advisable to interest boys and girls in language study, as if they were engaged in a kind of game, and make them imitate what the teacher says and does. Thought is very elusive and it is only by constant repetition on the part of a teacher that his pupils can secure the expression of it within their brains. The following process may be helpful to language teachers in bringing about a good effect in their class work :

7

Teacher's Preparation
{
1. Looking at (or reading about) the subject of lesson.
2. Remembrance in correct order.
3. Imagination of the scene.
}

Actual lesson 40 or 50 minutes.
{
1. Give the title of the lesson.
2. Description of the scene.
3. Sentences of the text *in Japanese*.
4. Verbs—*in Japanese* with gestures.
5. Call attention.
6. Teach the verbs in the foreign language —each three or four times carefully, with gestures.
7. Recitation on the part of students (This is for the verbs only : afterwards will come the building up of the whole sentences.)
}

Foreign words must be pronounced at least six or seven times in all ;—slowly at first and then quickly, so that pupils can master them properly. It is often found better to do this 3 times first, and then again 3 times, with one final repetition,—making seven times—and not all at once.

2nd Hour.

LESSON II.

I GO HOME.

Scene : The school ; then the student's own home.

Verbs.	Complete Sentences.
open	I open the door.
go out	I go out of the room.

8

turn	I turn round.
put out	I put out my hand.
push	I push the door.
turn	I turn the handle.
shut	I shut the door.
go	I go home.
sit	I sit down.
eat	I eat some food.
drink	I drink some tea.
write	I write my lessons.

TEACHER'S AND PUPILS' SENTENCES.

I am going to teach these verbs.
It is your turn.
Speak, please.
I am listening.
Go on.
Don't be afraid.
Very good indeed!
Excellent!
You speak very good English.
You flatter me.
Not at all.

NOTES.

Four pronunciations of " O." With characteristic names.

1. O¹ ▱ " High-collar " o (*Special to English*).

2. ō ▭ broad o.

3. □ Something like Japanese o.

4. ◁ deep " funnel " o.

9

Examples short and long : (1) not, log (2) bought, law (3) police, obey (4) boat, slow.

Three pronunciations of " Your."

Yuu-ɛ (pedantic), Yō-ɛr or Yōɛ (ordinary), Yɛ (quick).

3rd Hour.

READING.

From Scott's " Ivanhoe."

Method the same as on the preceding day.

~~~~~~~~~~~~

THE THIRD LECTURE.

1st Hour.

ON THE TEACHING OF LANGUAGES.

(The writer absented himself from the school on this day; but the outline of Mr. Swan's lecture is said to be as follows.)

That there are several different methods of teaching languages, but a lack of good introductory books.

That for beginners the scenes of Japanese life should in English first be taught, and afterwards English scenes in English.

That grammar should not be taught by itself but ought to be taught always along with other lessons.

That Eastern literature should be studied in English.

That English literature of two classes should be studied:— That which expresses facts of English life and that which is beautiful or noble.

10

Various suggested exercises.

(1st) TRUTH (FACTS).   (2nd) BEAUTY.

LITERARY COMPOSITION ON THE LESSONS.

Reading Aloud.   Reciting.   Elocution.   Plays.
Speeches. Dialogues. Original Essays.   Short
Stories. Dramas. Poems. Fables.

2nd Hour.

SEQUENCES OF ACTIONS.

LESSON III.

I GO TO ENGLAND.

**Scene: Tokyo ; Yokohama harbour;
a train, the steamboat.**

VERBS.	COMPLETE SENTENCES.
pack	I pack up my things.
call	I call a jinrikisha.
go	I go to Shimbashi Station.
take	I take a train.
go	I go to Yokohama.
take	I take a small boat.
go on	I go on board a ship.
starts	The ship starts.
sails	The ship sails.
steams	The ship steams 12 days.
arrives	The ship arrives at Vancouver.
land	I land at Vancouver.
cross	I cross America by a train.
arrives	I arrive at New York.
stay	I stay a few days in New York.

3rd Hour.

READING.

From Scott's "Ivanhoe." Method same as the preceding.

THE FOURTH LECTURE.

1st Hour.

ON THE TEACHING OF ENGLISH.

Mr. Swan, in his usual good humor, came on the platform and began his lecture in a clear loud voice. Imagination—the power of seeing pictures in the mind—he said, is used in this system in connection with simple correct English idioms. The sound of the idiom is associated with the imagined picture or scene : example :—To "wake up" is associated with a bedroom and various early morning sounds. Only the most usual correct idiomatic sentences should be taught first—those in use among all educated English people. This importance of selecting right sentences should be taken notice of by teachers of English. In Japan, Æsop's Fables and other books of similar kind are in vogue among beginners of English. It is undeniable that these books are of great value from the standpoint of literature, since they go far in improving one's character ; but as text-books for language study, they are scarcely to be recommended. Teachers should rather choose books written in habitual and common language, not the ones of untrue stories, even though they convey sound morals, as found in fables, allegories, etc. Base your sentences on facts which are linked together by time ; such sentences are sure to go into the brains of little folks more effectively, more precisely and more lastingly than figurative ones. For instance, such clauses as " I get up in the morning," or " I take my breakfast " are commonly used and are therefore easily learned by children. Idioms when chosen should be put into the order of nature. The best order of teaching habitual idioms is that of sequence in time. Technical terms, poetical words and familiar colloquialisms or slang, if taught at all, should be taught after pupils have mastered the common correct idioms.

Verbs are explained with advantage by gestures and then their meanings are impressed by repetition of their pronunciation. The professor proved the efficiency of this system by his personal examples, taking different verbs from a series of sentences relating to a blacksmith.

2nd Hour.
PRONUNCIATION OF WELL KNOWN RHYMES.

" Hark, hark the dogs do bark,
The beggars are coming to town,
Some in rags and some in jags,
And some in a velvet gown.
Some give them white bread,
Some give them brown,
Some give them plumcake,
And send them out of town."

The above is one of the popular nursery rhymes which, with other similar kinds of sentences, furnish good matter for practising pronunciation or for learning by heart. Being well known to every English child, it is very easy to find out whether the pronunciation be correct or not.

13

LESSON IV.

I GO TO ENGLAND—(*Continued*).

Scene: Atlantic steamboat. Southampton, London.

VERBS.	COMPLETE SENTENCES.
am	I am in New York.
leave	I leave New York.
starts	The boat starts.
steams	The boat steams.
crosses	The boat crosses the Atlantic Ocean.
arrives	The boat arrives at Southampton.
go	I go on board the steam launch.
land	I land at Southampton.
get into	I get into a train.
starts	The train starts.
goes	The train goes very fast.
passes	The train passes many stations.
slows	The train slows down.
stops	The train stops at Waterloo Station.
get out	I get out of the train.
call	I call a porter.
looks after	The porter looks after my luggage.
calls	The porter calls a cab.
put	He put the luggage on the cab.
get into	I get into the cab.
drives	The cabman drives the cab.
stops	The cab stops at a hotel.
get out	I get out of the cab.
ask	I ask the cabman, " How much ? "
pay	I pay the cabman.
go into	I go into the hotel. ·

14

NOTES.

" Hotel," " Address," " Correct," are the words derived from the French, and the accent is on the last syllable.

3rd Hour.

READING.

From Scott's " Ivanhoe." The method as already mentioned.

THE FIFTH LECTURE.

1st Hour.

ON THE TEACHING OF ENGLISH.

Before beginning the lecture, Mr. Swan suggested to the students to form an organization in order to increase their energy and mutually to procure all possible benefit therefrom during the time that the assembly continued. He made one more suggestion as to the compilation of an English dictionary with exact pronunciation. Concerning this, he said that we should take a small dictionary and, dividing its pages among us, mark the pronunciation of words in the new phonetic signs he was intending to give. Thus, the exertion of 110 intelligent students would in a short time bring the work to a satisfactory end. He also said that he was then engaged in a similar task himself, but that it would take him a long time to finish it. He then dealt with the problem of speaking.

In Japan, most English scholars devote themselves exclusively to reading literary works; in fact they are well versed in English literature, but only a few of them can speak the tongue properly. More attention should be paid to speaking and to the means of acquiring the useful art of, how to speak properly. People of all social ranks have their own way of speaking; so by listening to a man speaking, we can judge whether he is vulgar or noble, educated or uneducated. Hence comes the important question of selecting expressions.

The kinds of English that Japanese students should acquire are (1) Educated gentlemen's English, (2) Business English, (3) College Student's English. When we read books, especially novels, we must take special notice of the different expressions used by different characters, and learn to what kind of English people they belong. This will greatly help us to acquire good English. To those of the primary grade, 200 common practical English idioms would suffice to enable them to carry on a very simple ordinary conversation, provided those 200 idioms are so thoroughly practised that they are easily expressed in case of necessity.

Teach your pupils six or seven of such colloquial sentences every day, arranging them in accordance with habitual actions; and let the sentences be frequently repeated. If thus taught, the pupils will be able to master a large number of idioms in time, without fear of forgetting them.

Further explanation was made as to the method of teaching idiomatic sentences. The outline of his opinion was as follows:

Pick out verbs first, and make gestures and oral explanations. Gestures seen by pupils' eyes, and sounds heard by their ears, make the impression stronger by association.

Exaggerate the sounds of principal words in reciting sentences. Repeat them slowly once or twice, then more

16

quickly by degrees. In explaining concrete nouns, (such as looking-glass, snail, hammer, postman, etc.) you must appeal to the pupils' senses and also make proper gestures ; if images are clearly formed in your own brain, you can carry them to children's brains in this way.

2nd Hour.

SEQUENCES OF ACTIONS.

LESSON V.

WAKING UP AND BREAKFASTING.

Scene : a bedroom ; a dining room.

VERBS.	COMPLETE SENTENCES.
wake up	I wake up in the morning at six o'clock.
wash	I wash myself in cold water.
dress	I dress myself.
go down	I go down stairs.
go in	I go into the dining room.
sit down	I sit down at a table.
eat	I eat my breakfast.

TEACHER'S AND PUPILS' SENTENCES.

Can you imagine ?
Do your best !
Please say the next verb.
Very good ! Excellent !
You speak very good English.
You flatter me.
Not at all.

17

3rd Hour.

READING.

From Scott's " Ivanhoe." The same method of teaching as previously described.

NOTES.

Literature.—No English student should neglect the study of English masterpieces. Noble thoughts, beautiful ideas and all good customs of the past generations are embodied in English literature. Improve your character by the perusal of such works.

Pronunciation.—To pronounce the article " a " when in a sentence, like *ay* (in pay) is pedantic, and is limite to preachers or other public speakers, though common among Americans; ă is preferable. When it stands by itself, however, it is usually pronounced " ay."

~~~~~~~~~~

THE SIXTH LECTURE.

1st Hour.

ON THE TEACHING OF ENGLISH.

This morning, Prof. Swan began his lecture by reaffirming the necessity of teaching common English idioms to an elementary class; of choosing normal sentences; and of avoiding untrue sentences because of misleading innocent children,—the subject which formed a principal part of

18

his first hour's lecture of the preceding day. He further added that it requires some practice and the culture of imagination on the part of a language teacher to make his lesson full of colour and thus prevent his pupils from becoming tired.

We are apt to look down on simple sentences with contempt, but they are, in reality, very difficult to write. Even first-rate English authors, who write excellent compound or complex sentences, find it hard to express their ideas in a plain, simple style,—and much more so with these to whom English is not a mother tongue.

There are, he said, a number of good books, in which we can acquire model simple styles. Among the rest, he recommended Andersen's "Fairy Tales," "Grimm's Goblins," and also the study of the Bible for the purpose,—Proverbs, Psalms and Matthew in particular.

Next, he referred to the ancient teaching method of Confucius, which was as follows :

1st Year. The study of manners and customs.
2nd Year. The study of public speaking.
3rd Year. The study of history and politics.
4th Year. The study of perfection of style.

This ancient order, he said, is of great advantage in acquiring linguistic knowledge.

2nd Hour.

PRACTICE LESSON.

One of those who attended the lecture, Mr. Yoshikawa by name, asked the professor if he might now try to make a lesson on sequences of actions. This request having been granted, the enthusiastic student proceeded to give a very vivacious lesson which was criticised and properly corrected. The lesson was as follows :—

SEQUENCES OF ACTIONS.

LESSON VI.

WASHING HANDS.

Scene: a lodging house : a well.

VERBS.	COMPLETE SENTENCES.
have been cleaning	I have been cleaning a lamp-chimney.
are	My hands are dirty.
go out	I go out of the house.
take hold	I take hold of the bucket by the handle.
draw	I draw some water.
pour out	I pour out some water into the basin.
put back	I put back the bucket into the well.
soap	I soap my hands.
wash	I wash my hands.
take	I take a towel.
wipe	I wipe my hands with the towel.
are clean	My hands are now clean.

3rd Hour.

Mr. Yoshikawa, the bold volunteer of the preceding hour, made a new request for a full explanation of the game of cricket. Prof. Swan asked the whole class whether they had the same desire. Finding the request was almost unanimously seconded, the lecturer gave a

20

practical explanation of this national game of England in a humorous way, with a base ball and an improvised bat.

~~~~~~~~~~

THE SEVENTH LECTURE.

1st Hour.

ON PHONETICS.

As soon as morning greetings were interchanged, Prof. Swan wrote on the blackboard the three following sentences, " It is very wet to-day," " It is raining," " I hope it will soon clear up."

He then remarked that every teacher of language should always be attentive to pupils' state of mind, and utilize it, when necessity demands, stopping his regular lesson for two or three minutes.

For instance, on such a rainy day as this, he said, all the pupils' minds are sensitive to the disagreeable weather ; so it is advantageous to give 2 or 3 sentences on the weather to please children, who will well recite and memorise them. Thus the monotony for the moment being broken, their minds are quite ready to turn to regular lessons. Prof. Swan next wrote the three simple sentences which are given above, in phonetic signs thus, " It i : z vé-ri wĕt tu dè : i," " It i : z rĕ : ining," " Aai нǝ : up it wi : ɛl suu : n kliia-r-œp."

He now proceeded to the subject for the day, namely phonetics and indicated the total number of different simple vowel sounds contained in the English language by phonetic symbols as follows.

21

SHORT SOUNDS.		LONG SOUNDS.	
1 Æ (æ)	cat, pack.	Æ :	bag, cab, man.
2 O^A (o^a)	pot, hot.	O^A :	dog, god, fond.
3 Ō (ō)	bought, caught.	Ō :	broad, law.
4 Œ (œ)	cut, up.	Œ :	run, dug, love, come.
5 A (a)	*a* door, idea.	A :	a—door (*slowly*).
6 Aa (open)	cast, chance.	Aa :	father, calm, rather.
7 é (closed)	get, wet.	é :	bed, beg, men.
8 è (open)	wherefore.	è :	pear, pair; pay (pè:i).
9 i	bit, it.	i :	big, hid, begin.
10 ii (compressed)	beat, sheep.	ii :	read, feed, tea.
11 o	police.	o :	obey, (*rare*).
12 ⊙ (deep)	coat, boat.	⊙ :	grow, know, load.
13 u (flat)	book, foot.	u :	good, would, wood.
14 uu (round)	root, boot.	uu :	rude, food, wooed.
15 ε the; Englishman, garden,	cotton, pencil (*quickly*).	ε :	silvern, the — door. (*similar to 16*).
16 oε fir-tree, earth, hurt.		oε :	burn, world, word, turn, learn.

In all, 32 vowels—16 short, long. Many vowels said
to be short by the dictionaries, are really long, as shown
in the above list. The first four sounds are special to
English.

NOTES.

"Day" is pronounced "daai" by vulgar people. Education changes pronunciation, sometimes too much : for
example, the "Nε-uu rii:aa-li" of aristocratic affected pronunciation (No, really?). The length of sounds may be
shown by a teacher in class, by putting the hands farther
from or nearer to each other. (| |) or ⟨||).

22

2nd Hour.

Prof. Swan first gave full particulars about a European dining room with illustrations, and then gave a lesson on sequences of actions.

SEQUENCES OF ACTIONS.

LESSON VII.

BREAKFAST.

Scene : a dining room of a hotel.

VERBS.	COMPLETE SENTENCES.
take	I take a seat.
comes	The waiter comes.
order	I·order my breakfast (ham and eggs).
bring	The waiter brings the dish and sets it down
sets down	on the table.
lift off	The waiter lifts off the cover.
take	I take a knife and fork.
eat	I eat my breakfast.

After the lecture, more than fifty of the teachers who attended the summer school held, at the Fujimiken restaurant on Kudan, a dinner party to which Prof. and Mrs. Swan and a Japanese friend of the former's were invited. At this meeting, a lecture on table manners was given by Prof. Swan. The etiquette recommended by him was well observed by all his hosts to his great delight. After dinner, Mrs. Swan and the professor's friend delivered

23

speeches respectively on "Japanese ladies," and "The method of teaching foreign languages in Germany." Two or three teachers spoke in Japanese of their experiences in language teaching. Upon the suggestion of the professor, a plan for organizing an English teachers' association was proposed, but being an important question, it was left for further debate. The party dispersed at nearly half-past four p. m.

THE EIGHTH LECTURE.

1st Hour.

ON PREPOSITIONS AND SUBJECTIVE LANGUAGE.

Prof. Swan delivered first a simple lecture on the method of teaching together sentences of the objective language (facts) and the subjective language (thoughts and emotions), promising to give the details further on. He then went on to the lecture on prepositions.

The essential words used in constructing a sentence are verbs and nouns, all other parts of speech being dependent upon these two. Prepositions are, like the rest, sometimes a part of a verb (as up, down, out, in, etc.) and at other times they are really a part of a noun (as at, upon, over, etc.); or else they belong in some cases to one and sometimes to the other (examples, put on a hat, put on the table, get round an official, go round a house). The best way of mastering the use of prepositions is to get into the habit of considering the various prepositions as

24

the different names given to distances or air spaces. He then explained the true meanings of the following prepositions by means of his ingenious gestures.

THE VARIOUS AIR SPACES BETWEEN OBJECTS.

On—pressing down.
At—touching sideway.
From—an increasing air space.
By—sideway, but not touching.
To—movement to a certain point.
Towards—going round to or at a distance.
Off—downwards movement away from.
Of—part of, still sticking to.
In—movement to a hollow.
Into—movement inside from outside.
Unto—at to (old fashioned).
Among—at mingled.
Amongst—same as among (usually with "the.")
Round—circular movement.
Around—at parts of a circle.
About—from centre to different directions (at by out).
Over—high up.
Above—higher still (at by over).
Across—from side to side.
Under—looking down ⊔.
Underneath—covered up ⊔.
Beneath—at several points under ||||| or stretched
    under ≡.
Below—lower than under ⊥
Away—along a path to a distance ——→ ·····
Away from—along a path from a certain point ·····——→

25

Far away from—very long path.
Near—small air space.
Near to—small particular place.
Far—very long air space.
Close—very small space.
Close to—very small, some particular place.
With—hand in hand.
Along with—some distance hand in hand.
Side by side with—like two friends walking together.
Abreast of—like soldiers two by two.
Alongside—like two sleepers, or a ship in a dock.
Upon—high up and on.
Between—by two (inside two), " by twain."

2nd Hour.

" The Method of teaching Modern Languages in Germany," by Miss Brebner, was recommended by the professor, as a book of reference as to various methods of teaching foreign languages in the Occident. In European countries, he said, children are taught naturally by mothers first in intonation, pronunciation and then the separation of words, which is followed by writing and reading. Saying this, he recited the following nursery rhymes as examples of verses commonly known by English children.

" The evening red
And the morning gray,
Are two good signs
Of a very fine day."

" Rain before seven,
Clear up before eleven."

26

SEQUENCES OF ACTIONS.

LESSON VIII.

ENGLISH STUDENT'S LIFE.

Scene : an English student's room.

VERBS.	COMPLETE SENTENCES.
asleep	A student is asleep in his bed.
ring	The bell rings at six in the morning.
wakes up	The student wakes up.
stretches	He stretches himself.
yawns	He yawns once or twice.
get up	And gets up quickly.
takes	He takes a cold bath.
rubs	He rubs himself.
dresses	He dresses himself partly.
exercises	He exercises himself.
finishes	He finishes dressing : he dresses himself.
goes down	Then he goes down to breakfast.

3rd Hour.

READING.

From " Flashes from the Far East," Part VII—First Impressions. 1—Arrival. About 2 pages. The method was changed from this day. The students each read a paragraph, the professor correcting their pronunciation, accentuation and intonation.

THE NINTH LECTURE.

1st Hour.

ON THE SUBJECTIVE LANGUAGE.

Prof. Swan came on the platform with an attitude apparently ready for the deliverance of a great lecture. And indeed the students' expectation was not belied, for he evinced the ability of an accomplished lecturer on this morning more than on any other day since the opening of this summer school. The writer's feeble pen can scarcely trace all the philosophical ideas, historical references and ethical explanations contained in this enthusiastic lecture, which was made with a rare eloquence. The following is only an outline of this lecture. The study of objective language undeniably forms a prominent part in the acquisition of linguistic knowledge. In consequence, a student of foreign languages should be acquainted with all the objective facts of life, manners and customs of the people who speak the tongue. But the study of these substantial items alone is liable to make one a materialist. Something higher and nobler must be studied. It is human nature to entertain a strong desire for all that is great, lofty and noble in quality, and nothing is greater, loftier and nobler than the elevated thoughts and sublime ideas of great men. It is this love of noble thoughts that laid the early foundation of ancient Greek civilization and that brought about the modern enlightenment of the west. Confucius, Mencius and other great Chinese philosophers have for the same reason had very many worshippers in the East. The universal influence of Christianity is also ascriba-

28

ble to the reverential attachment of the human mind to the noble doctrines of Christ. Thus, it is plain that a man's heart is naturally open to inspirations of noble quality and that he is ever ready to improve his character by the sound precepts of great men. The ultimate aim of language study should be based on the desire or determination of developing the noble sides of humanity, through the medium of great literary productions.

The English language takes pride in instilling the true meanings of such virtues as :—

> Justice, Honesty, Nobility, Truthfulness, Faithfulness, Kindness, Wisdom, Power, Love, etc..

The way to lead a man to noble life is to search for noble thoughts. Now, noble thoughts are invariably expressed in noble words which, when in constant use, must eventually lead to noble actions. Subjective language treats of the expressions of thoughts and aims at the improvement of character. But before dealing with the higher and nobler thoughts of a people, it is necessary to know one or two thousand of the usual idioms during the early years. Prof. Swan then suggested to his pupils the following order of teaching subjective language.

1. Creating the feeling in pupils' hearts.
2. Give Japanese idioms corresponding to English idioms.
3. The literal translation of English idioms.
4. Pick out principal words.
5. Teach these words, if possible giving vivid picture.
6. Teach other words. Try to find objective base for the symbol.

29

7. Give three or four examples specially chosen for suitability.

As an example of teaching simple subjective language, he explained the sentences written below.

1. Be quick.
2. Can you remember?
3. Don't lose time!
4. I will help you.
5. Patience, patience!

2nd Hour.

SEQUENCES OF ACTIONS.

LESSON IX.

LIGHTING A FIRE.

Scene: a drawing room, a fire-place.

VERBS.	COMPLETE SENTENCES.
stoops	The maid servant stoops down.
takes	She takes some wood.
puts in	She puts some wood in her apron.
carries	She carries some wood to the hearth-stone.
rakes out	She rakes out the ashes from the fire-place.
lays	She lays some crumpled paper in the fire-place.
places	She places some wood on the crumpled paper.
takes out	She takes out a match.
strikes	She strikes the match.
lights	She lights the fire.
burns	The fire burns.

TEACHER'S AND PUPILS' SENTENCES.

Can you remember ?   Don't lose time !
I will help you.
Be quick !   Make haste !
Very good pronunciation.
But rather slow.
Next time, be a little quicker.
This time it is much better !

3rd Hour.

READING.

From " Flashes from the Far East."
Continuance of the day before.   About 2 pages.
Another familiar rhyme among English children was taught, for the sake of the pronunciation.

> " Multiplication is vexation,
>   Division is as bad,
>   The rule of three, it puzzles me,
>   But practice drives me mad."

THE TENTH LECTURE.

1st Hour.

ON THE TEACHING OF GRAMMAR.

Prof. Swan's lecture on this morning was to be in relation to the method of teaching the English grammar in middle schools.   But previous to giving this lecture, he criticised the methods of language teaching now prevalent in our middle schools.

His first remark was on the wrong selection of text-books on English in our middle schools. The value of text-books lies in their being true, interesting, useful and idiomatic, while there are threads of thought running through them. Now, we can easily see that most text-books, " Readers " in particular, commonly adopted in middle schools, are all wanting in several of these points. Imperfect books must be changed for the perfect as soon as possible. But are there any recommendable books at present for the use of middle school students? Very few! Consequently, it is of imperative need to put into publication, text-books which are based on the best method of learning English. Then the professor remarked that Japanese teachers of English must improve themselves before using new text-books, so as to be ready for teaching the language in accordance with the newest and the most improved methods. Moreover, they must ever be careful to make their teaching interesting, and thus keep their pupils from weariness. It is possible for an able language teacher to make usually uninteresting lessons—say, spelling—interesting. The following nursery rhyme is absurd and nonsensical, but in some way it can be converted into a good and interesting lesson.

> A spit stood up like a lusty man,
> And vowed he'd kill the dripping pan.
> " Ods tuts ! " said the gridiron,
> " Can't you agree ?
> I'm the head constable,
> Bring him to me ! "

As good as his word, he made this lesson actually

32

interesting by comparing the spit (a piece of sharp iron)
to a sharp person employed in a merchant's office, the drip-
ping pan to some one who was too fond of money, and the
gridiron to the merchant or manager. It was then given in
dramatic and forcible manner with accurate pronunciation.

Next, he came to the grammar, criticising its present
method of teaching from the lowest course to the highest.
His opinion was that it is quite useless, nay, often harmful
to cram pupils' brains with difficult, indigestib'e rules of
grammar. The aim of grammar is the perfecting of style,
and this belongs to a college course. At present too much
time is devoted to the study of this subject in middle schools,
so that really little good result comes from it. To speak
and write in ordinary English correctly is effected more
by practice and habit rather than by grammatical rules.
If grammar is to be taught at all, care must be taken
not to puzzle the young minds with such rules as are
regarded as out-of-the-way. Grammatical knowlege should
be obtained from readîng and writing, not from grammar
itself, and the rules which are found useful by the students
in their daily practice in speaking should be collected
and put into a small book. Thus the principal rules, instead
of having to be learned, are already known by practice. In
an elementary course, the parts of speech should be taught
in simple sentences, in such a way as to let pupils get
an idea of the two great essential parts—verbs and nouns —
all other words as being parts of them. Here the lecturer
referred to the present method of teaching composition,
saying that it is very unnatural to tax pupils' brains by or-
dering them to compose on a certain topic given by a teacher.
To give a child a dictionary, grammar and an exercise book

33

and tell him to write good idiomatic English, he said, is just as if one should give a carpenter silver, brass and steel, and tell him to play the part of watch-maker. To speak and write English requires skill, and this must necessarily be begun in imitation.

Give your pupils some good English sentences and make them reproduce the same sentences exactly in speaking first and then in reading and writing while their memory is still active.

It is in this way that children begin to learn how to speak, read and write. In conclusion, Prof. Swan suggested that hand-writing should always be begun by capital letters, first in printing forms and then gradually in scripts, as :—

CAT   cat   *cat*   *cat*

With regard to suitable stories for boys to read, Henty's novels, (of which there are twenty in all,) were recommended as written in a good and simple style.

2nd Hour.

No lesson, all having sat for a photograph.

3rd Hour.

READING.

From " Flashes from the Far East," Yokohama Station. About 3 pages. Method as already described.

THE ELEVENTH LECTURE.

1st Hour.

ON TEACHING THE ENGLISH ALPHABET AND THE ENGLISH LANGUAGE TO BEGINNERS.

Before beginning the lecture, Prof. Swan made a reference to the weather, writing on the board, " It is rather dull to day." (It i : z raa : dhɛ dœ-ɛl tu-dè : i) which sentence was recited by the students several times. The lecturer then declared that every serious teacher of language should ask himself, " What text-books must be used by his pupils ? " The solution of this question means success in language teaching ; but unfortunately few have ever properly settled this question. The Educational Department, language scholars and publishers have written abundant text-books without much consulting young readers as to their tastes. The result is that children are dissatisfied with these insipid books, as they think, and lose heart for the study of language. The question of publishing appropriate text-books on the study of foreign languages can not indeed be too seriously considered. The selection of daily lessons, too, is required to be accompanied with some pains on the part of a teacher. The motto is " Find out from pupils what kind of lesson they like best." From among a list of lessons which the pupils like, a teacher should choose one and make a discourse on it.

The professor himself then asked his pupils of what subjects they would like him to speak, and was immediately given the following suggestions :—" English student," " English court," " Popular reading books," " Phonetics," " Tenses of verbs," " Farm yard," " Going to the city," " Etiquette," " English child and mother," " Orator," " Popular songs," " Dress and costume," " Station," " Hotel," and " Shop." The professor did not, of course, make a choice at once of these manifold subjects to speak about, the question itself having been asked for example's sake. His suggested order of Teaching Absolute Beginners was then written out as follows :—

1. Make a list of subjects suitable.
2. Teach the oral part first.
3. Tell the pupils a story of the subject chosen.
4. Let the pupils tell you the same story in Japanese.
5. Write the story in Japanese or make notes of the chief words.
6. Pick out verbs first.
7. The teacher translates the verbs into English.
8. The teacher translates the nouns into English.
9. The teacher repeats the verbs and nouns in English.
10. The teacher examines the pupils.
11. The teacher teaches the letters needed—using only capital letters for No. 1 lesson.
12. The teacher writes some words on the blackboard.
13. The pupils copy them.
14. The pupils read their copies.
15. The pupils read their books (note : at the end of all.)

36

16. The pupils go home and copy the lessons neatly.

2nd Hour.

SPECIMEN LESSON TO ABSOLUTE BEGINNERS.

Porf. Swan said with an accurate pronunciation "Fan," at the same time, showing a fan in his hand, and made his pupils pronounce the word several times. He then said "Hand," also showing his hand, the repetition of the students following as before. The words "Have," "I," "In," "My," "A" were also practised separately. Then these words were composed one by one till they made a sentence, "I have a fan in my hand." This sentence was repeated by the professor five or six times, slowly first and then quicker by degrees, each time followed by the students. The next sentence, "A man is on a horse," was likewise practiced, the professor making each word the more intelligible by his clever pictures and skillful gestures. He then represented the sounds of each word by the pictorial letters of his system, gradually changing them into Roman letters, as shown below.

M A N H O R S E

HAND   MY   FAN   IS

A MAN ON A HORSE.
A MAN IS ON A HORSE.
A FAN.
A FAN IN A HAND.
A FAN IS IN MY HAND.
I HAVE A FAN IN MY HAND.

The professor explained this method of teaching alphabet, associating sounds with various drawings of the mouth or of objects which represent the sound.

Order of Teaching The Alphabet.

1. Interest the pupils in the subject.
2. Show objects, or drawings of them.
3. Pronounce distinctly many times, at the same time associating the sounds with objects.
4. Repeat this after a short interval.
5. Examine the students.
6. Take one word and analyse the sounds.
7. Choose parts of the mouth, or suitable objects to represent the separate sounds.
8. Draw these objects on the board.
9. Do the same for other words.

38

10. Construct the sentences in the English order.
11. Write the sentences in pictorial signs.
12. Make the students either read their own copies or · the sentences on the board.
13. Write again in English capital letters.
14. Make the students read the capital letters.
15. Make the students copy the capital letters.
16. Make the students read their copies.
17. Finally show the students the book printed in capital letters.

By this method, it takes 50 minutes in speaking and 10 in reading, but the pronuncation of the pupils is absolutely correct, if the teacher's is correct.

A book was recommended for· teaching the game of cricket, with illustrations of the correct attitudes.
" Cricket for Beginners "—by A.C. MacLaren, published by Routledge, price 50 cents. Also the description in " Scenes of English Life," Part III.

3rd Hour.

Having been unanimously requested to sing an English song, the professor sang "Rule Britannia" in a fine baritone.

RULE BRITANNIA—(TRUE VERSION).

When Britain first, at Heav'n's command,

Arose from out the azure main,
This was the charter, the charter of the land,
And guardian angels sang the strain :
(Chorus) Rule, Britannia,

Britannia rules the Waves,
Britons never, never, never,
Shall be slaves!

RULE BRITANNIA—(SAILORS' VERSION.)

(1) 'Twas in the Atlantic Ocean,
At the equinotical gales,
That a man of ours fell overboard
Amongst the sharks and whales.
(Chorus) Sing, Rule Britannia.

(2) His ghost appeared at my bed side
Saying, Weep no more for me,
I am married to a mermaid
At the bottom of the deep blue sea.
(Chorus).........................

This latter version, he said, is sung at English boys' schools.

Again, a practical explanation on the game of cricket, the professor almost forgetting the scorching heat of the mid-day sun in his earnest practical illustration.

———

After school, a meeting was opened in the Hall, with the purpose of considering the means of reforming the current methods of teaching English in middle and normal schools.

Professor Swan and almost all the students attended the meeting, which was presided over by one of the elder students. The debate was mostly connected with the question how far the new method lectured upon by Prof. Swan was practically adoptable in the intermediate educational world.

THE TWELFTH LECTURE.

1st Hour.

ON GRAMMAR (SIMPLE TENSES OF VERBS.)

Prof. Swan, as will be learned by his previous lectures, is in opposition to the teaching of grammar by itself. He dwelt more at length this morning upon this particular branch of language study. He is of opinion that the mastery of all difficult grammatical rules and terms does not necessarily make one approach the two great goals of linguistic study, namely—to speak and to write correctly. The average Englishman cannot name all kinds of moods and tenses of verbs, and may not even know such grammatical terms as common Japanese students have by heart. Nevertheless, the former speaks and writes so admirably by habit and practice that the latter can hardly expect to reach to his standard with all their grammatical knowledge. It is not of course fair to look at the Japanese, to whom English is an adopted tongue, in the same light as English people. The point is that the Japanese' as the European people do, should acquire the English language as far as possible on a natura method; in other words, by habit and practice. Then Prof. Swan explained how we can simplify the teaching of simple tenses of verbs and make pupils get a clear conception of practical rules in them, as every English child does unconsciously.

"A photographer's shop," he said, "may be taken to represent a brain with all its images." Then, as a photographer arranges his photographs, so the brain arranges its images in sets of the same kind together. Any box of photographs contains many of the same kinds. One box has photos of *jinrikishas*, and another those of flowers and so forth. The photographer can find any photo at once by looking for it. The clever man can do the same and bring up any image at once directly the word is spoken."

Diagram of Tenses: Simple Action.

YESTERDAY.	TODAY.		TOMORROW.
I	have	am	will
he	has	is	—
you —ed	have —ed	are —ing	shall —

Symbolic Grammar Chart.

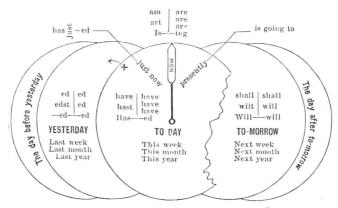

INVENTED BY MESSRS H. SWAN AND V. BÉTIS.

A teacher would do well to make a list of irregular verbs and compose a short story of it to interest his pupils. Example, a three-volume story :—

1st Volume.

flies, is, sees, raises, aims, pulls, shoots, hits, falls.

This series of verbs represents in brief the action of a sportsman with his gun. The bird rises and the sportsman shoots.

2nd Volume.

Whistles, comes, runs, sniffs, search-es, finds, brings, stoops, looks at, feels, opens, puts in.

Now the sportsman whistles to his dog and the dog goes after the bird. The dog finds the bird and brings it back. The sportsman, admiring the bird, puts it in his bag.

3rd Volume.

returns, goes in, sits down, receives, takes, sits down, plucks, cooks, car-ves, eat.

Next, the sportsman goes back home and gives the partridge or pheasant to his wife who plucks it, cooks it ; and they all eat. The smell of the cooked bird can almost be smelt by the students.

43

2nd Hour.

LESSON X.

SEQUENCES OF ACTIONS.

A PRACTICAL LESSON BY ONE OF THE STUDENTS.

CRITICISM BY PROF. SWAN.

A JAPANESE STUDENT DRESSES HIMSELF.

Scene : a Japanese student's room.

VERBS.	COMPLETE SENTENCES.
	It is seven o'clock in the morning.
shines	The sun shines into the room.
wakes up	The student wakes up.
stretches	He stretches himself.
yawns	He yawns once or twice.
sits up	He sits up.
takes off	He takes off his night gown.
reaches	He reaches his hand to his day gown.
pulls	He pulls the clothes to his side.
draws	He draws the clothes over his back.
passes	He passes his hands into the sleeves.
gets up	He gets up on his feet.
shakes	He shakes the flaps of his clothes.
puts on	He puts on the right flap first and then the left flap.
stoops	He stoops down.
picks up	He picks up his sash.
puts	He puts it round and round his waist.

44

3rd Hour.

READING.

From "Flashes from the Far East," Chap. VI, "Yokohama to Tokyo;" 3 pages. Method as usual, together with use of the "phonetic vowel chart."

THE THIRTEENTH LECTURE.

1st Hour.

ON THE TEACHING OF GRAMMAR.
(PRINCIPLES AND PRACTICE.)

This morning, Prof. Swan dealt with the principles and practice of the grammar on his system. His principles are as follows.

1. The pupil must be interested.

Dullness and monotony, which attend as a rule on the teaching of grammar, must first be surmounted; and the teacher must prepare his pupils' minds favourably for this lesson, as well as for all other branches of language study.

2. The lesson must be applied to the pupil himself, now or in future.

3. Apply the examples in the lesson to the student's own life.

These two principles purport to make grammar teaching full of life, attracting thereby the pupils' attention and interest to this particular lesson. For instance, instead of the dry examples on the subjunctive mood for which pupils have

45

no personal concern such as are usually found in a grammar book, if you would give three or four practical examples in direct relation to their daily life, the impression would not easily die out. Here Prof. Swan asked his pupils if there had been any one who had absented himself the day before; having got an affirmative reply from one corner, he gave a practical example of the *hypothetical* by saying "*If you had been* here yesterday, *you would have known* all about this lesson."

4. Use very simple grammar names.

Many of the grammatical terms are of foreign derivation and having ambiguous significations in them, they impose useless labor tasks for memorising. For instance, such terms as "noun," "tense" and "mood" should at first respectively be replaced in the early stages by words in daily use, such as "name," "time" and "manner." The following names may serve for the terms of simple tenses.

"I, this morning" (for 1st person, singular, present perfect) as, I have washed.

"We, yesterday" (for 1st person, plural, past) as, we washed.

"You, to-morrow" (for 2nd person, singular or plural, future) as, you will wash.

"He, everyday" (for 3rd person, singular, habitual present) as, he washes every morning.

"They, now" (for 3rd person, plural, present progressive) as, they are washing.

The technical grammatical terms are better left for a later stage in the course.

5. In the objective language, do not change the picture.

This is to prevent confusion of thought and to keep the pupils' active attention to one picture throughout the whole lesson.

6. In the subjective language, change the picture several times.

Words of abstract sense are only expected to be fully understood by young pupils when explanation is accompanied by three or four practical examples. Prof. Swan asked for three examples which might express the meaning of "hope," and got from his pupils the examples written below :—

"I hope the weather will soon clear up."

"One of my friends is now on the sick list, and I hope he will soon recover his former health

"We hope Professor Swan will publish some good text-books on English."

The professor also gave the examples of a man in a boat cast away on the sea—"He hopes to get safely to shore;" of a man entombed in a mine waiting for rescue—"He hopes to be saved;" of a mother sitting by a sick child—"She hopes her child will soon be well." As an interlude to the grammar, which had certainly been from its nature a hard lesson to follow to many of the students, the professor cheered up their spirits by giving another nursery rhyme for the sake of pronunciation, this time in the past potential mood (could).

"Jack Sprat
Could eat no fat,
And his wife could eat no lean,
And so, betwixt them both, you see
They licked the platter clean !"

In Phonetics :—(Jæ : k Spræ : t
 Cu : d ii : t no : u fæt.
End hiz waa : if cu : d ii : t
 no : u lii—n'
Ænd so : u, bitwikst dhém
 bo : uth yuu s ii:—
Dhèi likt dhɛ plætɛ klii : n.)

The application of this rhyme may be seen in such a sentence as, "One teacher teaches idiom and another grammar, and so betwixt them both, you see, the pupils will learn English."

The lecturer then resumed the problem of teaching grammar, this time on complex tenses, which were classified into four parts *i.e.* (1) short action, (2) every-day action, (3) long action and time, long and short action. These were explained by the following diagrams.

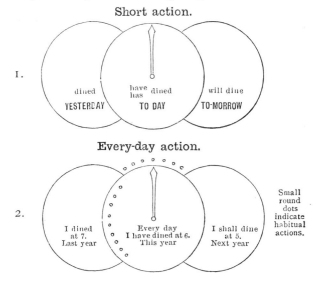

Long action and time.

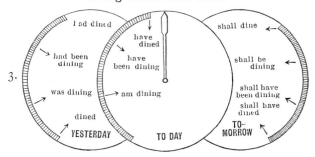

Long and short action.

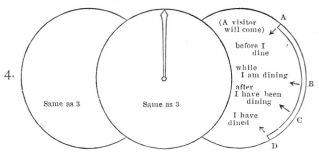

2nd Hour.
SEQUENCES OF ACTION.
LESSON XI.
GOING OUT IN A CAB.
Scene: a drawing room. The entrance of a hotel.

VERBS.	COMPLETE SENTENCES.
am	I am in a hotel.
go up	I go up to the bell.
ring	I ring the bell.
comes	The waiter comes.

49

say, want	I say to him, "Waiter, I want a cab."
goes	The waiter goes out.
calls	The waiter calls (or whistles) for a cab.
comes	The cab comes up to the door.
comes back	The waiter comes back.
say, is	He says to me, "Your cab is ready, sir."
take	I take my hat and umbrella.
put on	I put on my hat.
get out	I go out of the hotel.
get into	I get into the cab.
drive	I drive off.

3rd Hour.

READING.

From "Flashes from the Far East," Chap. VI, "Yokohama to Tokyo." About 3 pages. Method the same as on the preceding day.

THE FOURTEENTH LECTURE.

1st Hour.

ON COLLOQUIAL AND LITERARY ENGLISH.

Nursery rhymes are the means by which children learn pronunciation, intonation and an elementary conception of literature in their mother tongue. The following was a nursery rhyme which preceded the lecture on the topic given above.

50

" If all the world
Were bread and cheese,
And all the water, ink,
'T would make a parson
Scratch his head,
And go to bed and think."

Prof. Swan explained the philosophical meaning which
might be found in this rhyme, and trained his pupils in
pronunciation and modulation by it. He then entered up on
his lecture and expressed himself as follows: The study of
literature is one of the ultimate objects of linguistic acquisition.
Consequently, to learn how to speak and write in ordinary
language is the first step in language study. But many
students do not observe this order and they attempt to
speak a language by the study of literature, an attempt
which ends, of course, in failure. Students are therefore
required to shun all the literary masterpieces till they are
fairly well versed in customary expressions. Prof. Swan
extracted a few passages from Gray's " Elegy in a Country
Churchyard," pointing out therein words and phrases
which are not of daily use. The underlined are the expressions peculiar to the poet's character:

" The curfew *tolls* the *knell* of *parting day*,
The lowing herd *winds* slowly o'er the *lea*,
The ploughman homeward plods his *weary* way,
And leaves the world to darkness and to me.

Now *fades* the *glimmering landscape* on the sight,
And all the air a solemn stillness holds,
Save where the beetle *wheels* his *droning flight*
And *drowsy tinklings* lull the *distant folds*."

The professor added :—

" In the classical masterpieces of literature, it is impossible to be sure of the true sense of any word : the same word seems to be employed in a number of different meanings. These meanings are personal to the author and not inherent to the meaning of the word in its ordinary use. This it is, which explains why the usual study of classical authors cannot give the knowledge of the true sense of the word." Other examples were given by him. " Full many a flower is born to blush unseen," " The busy housewife plies her evening care "—where " born " strictly applies to a child, and " plies " to the shuttle of a loom. The lecturer then turned to the next point, ascribing peculiar literary expressions to three chief reasons :

1. A desire to use expressions different from habitual ones in order to produce novelty.

2. To give an appearance of life to inanimate objects, and the appearance of human personality to things and to qualities.

3. To produce a more vivid and striking effect by superposing mental pictures : sometimes even placing three mental pictures one behind the other, to create a lively stereoscopic effect in the mind of the reader.

2nd Hour.

The professor now gave the rules of giving a complete lesson as follows.

1. Title.

2. Scene—called up by means of short simple descriptions.

52

3. The corresponding Japanese sentences.
4. The Japanese verbs (that all pupils may understand.)
5. Call attention.
6. Teach the English verbs 3 times with gestures and some description *in Japanese.*
7. Stop and introduce conversational phrase or phrases.
8. Teach the verbs second time (each thrice).
9. Repeat the verbs third time (once, total 7).
10. Examine on the verbs by means of phrases of the subjective language.
11. Teach the nouns, constructing the sentences carefully in good order.
12. Conversational interlude.
13. Construct the sentences a second time with English details.
14. Repeat finally the full text of the lesson.
15. Examine by means of phrases, old and new (subjective language).
16. The students read, copy the sentences, and, if necessary, draw diagrams.

An experimental lesson was given by one of the students and duly criticised by Mr. Swan.

3rd Hour.

READING.

From " Flashes from the Far East," Chap. VII, " In the Train." About 3 pages. Method as already mentioned.

THE FIFTEENTH LECTURE.

1st Hour.

ON THE TEACHING OF LITERATURE.

The long continued wet weather turned out to be still worse this morning, it having been raining in regular torrents and chilly damp air filling the whole hall. Prof. Swan, little affected by the uncommon weather, wrote on the board, " What extraordinary weather we are having !" and pronounced the sentence in a clear loud voice three or four times, telling his pupils to follow him all together. Then he drilled them in pronunciation and 'intonation by giving another nursery rhyme, which is as follows :

" Thirty days hath September,
April, June and November;
February days are 28 alone,
All the rest have 31 ;
Except in Leap Year,
Then's the time
February days are 29."

Then the professor called the attention of the students to the study of character. He first described characters of inanimate objects, such as tree, iron and coal, etc. All these things, he said, have not permanent character, but always change. The character of the true man alone is permanent. Literary works are in reality the revelation of different characters of man. It is by the study of character that we can discover all hidden treasures in literature and thereby improve our own character. We can thus be more honest, truthful, wise and

54

kind. Words are expressive of character, and it is therefore important to notice carefully the varied phraseology which is found in literary works. For ordinary purposes, a student should be required to imitate the phraseology of English gentlemen, college professors and college students, studying at the same time their characters. It is a wonder to every English and American to hear Japanese students speak in English like one who has the combined character of a child, a philosopher, a telephone operator and a Macaulay. Certainly they must always be very careful to express themselves in accurate character, idiom and pronunciation. The professor then gave the order by which any lesson in Literature may profitably be taught.

1. Give the principal idea of the piece.
2. Describe the mental scene.
3. Expression of the text in colloquial language.
4. Construction of principal phrases on the verb first.
5. Construction of secondary phrases.
6. Construction in author's exact language and order.
7. Reconstruction of the whole passage.
8. Final repetition.
9. Recitation by pupils.
10. Author's technique should be observed (explanation on rhythm, choice of vowel, kind of consonant, alliteration, etc.)
11. Reading and copying.

Prof. Swan, as an example, taught a lesson in this order, taking as example a few passages from Gray's "Elegy." The text is as follows:

55

" The breezy call of incense-breathing morn,
The swallow twittering from the straw-built shed,
The cock's shrill clarion, or the echoing horn,
No more shall rouse them from their lowly bed.

No more for them the blazing hearth shall burn,
Nor busy housewife ply her evening care,
No children run to lisp their sire's return,
Nor climb his knees the envied kiss to share."

2nd Hour.

SEQUENCES OF ACTIONS.

LESSON XII.

CALLING ON A FRIEND.

**Scene : a drawing room, a street, a house
in European style.**

VERBS.	COMPLETE SENTENCES.
Take	I take a jinrickshaw.
go	I go to my friend's house.
get	I get to my friend's house.
take	I take out my card.
hand	I hand it to a servant.
takes	The servant takes it to his master.
looks	My friend looks at the card.
says, show	My friend says, " Show him in."
enter	I enter his room.
shake	I shake hands with my friend.
talk	We talk for a little while.
go	And then go to my friend's house in Yokohama.

56

LESSON XIII.

THE VISIT.

Scene : a station, a train, a European house, a river.

VERBS.	COMPLETE SENTENCES.
go	We go to the station.
take	We take our tickets.
get into	We get into a train.
goes	The train goes very fast.
stops	The train stops after a while.
get out	We get out of the train.
give up	We give up our tickets.
walk	We walk to my friend's house.
go in	We go in by the garden gate.
go up	We go up the steps.
go into	We go into the house.
take off	We take off our hats.
introduces	My friend introduces me to his wife.
offers	She offers her hand and says to me,
am pleased	" I am very pleased to see you."
have	" Will you have a cup of tea ? "
sit down	We sit down on the chairs in the veranda.
take	We each take a cup of tea.
says, would like, have	My friend says, " Would you like to have a row on the river ? "
row	We row on the river for a while.
come back	We come back home.
have	We have our dinner.

3rd Hour.

The school was over at 10 o'clock a.m. Consequently, no lesson on reading.

THE SIXTEENTH LECTURE.

1st Hour.

SUMMARY.

Prof. Swan's lecture on this morning was principally a summing up of all the lectures he had hitherto delivered; so its contents are not separately mentioned here. Let it suffice to say that the professor, among other matters which had already been stated, represented the tenses and moods of verbs by the different ways of playing with a " cup and ball." The manner of playing with this toy is to throw up the ball and catch it on the cup in various ways. The professor remarked that the same practice is needed to master the uses of tenses and moods as in playing with this simple plaything. "The different movements of the ball," he said.—" front, back, left, right and so on, for the same result, may be compared with indicative, potential, past, present, future, etc. To succeed, the *rule* is not sufficient, considerable *practice* is required."

2nd Hour.

SEQUENCES OF ACTIONS.

LESSON XIV.

ROWING.

Scene : a European house, a river.

VERBS.	COMPLETE SENTENCES.
go	I go from my friend's house to the water's edge.

58

drag	I drag the boat to the edge of the river.
launch	I launch the boat on the water.
get into	I get into the boat.
take	I take off my coat.
sit down	I sit down on the seat.
take	I take the oar.
row	I row the boat.

The Canadian boat song was added to the lesson:

" Row, brothers, row,
The stream runs fast,
The rapids are near,
And the daylight's past."

3rd Hour.

READING.

" Notes on English Literature " by Emery; " Rubaiyát of Omar Khayyám " by Fitzgerald; " Adventures of a Phaeton " by Black; and " Sherlock Holmes " by Conan Doyle, were recommended to the students. Prof. Swan wrote on the board a specimen passage from the " Rubaiyát of Omar Khayyám," and explained it according to his personal method. The first verse of that poem is as follows:

" Wake! For the Sun, who scattered into flight
The Stars before him from the field of Night,
Drives Night along with them from Heav'n, and strikes
The Sultán's turret with a shaft of Light."

Lesson in reading. From " Flashes from the Far East," Chap. VIII, " Shimbashi Station, Tokyo;" Chap. IX, " Skeegee." About 7 pages. Method as before.

THE SEVENTEENTH LECTURE.

1st Hour.

SUMMARY.

This day was the last of the Summer School, and the students, as may be imagined, were all attention to every word of Prof. Swan who, in his turn, seemed to put forth all his enthusiasm and energy in order to add a finishing touch to the discourses he had given. His first remark was with regard to his desire of introducing this psychological method to our middle schools at large. He admitted various hindrances which may lie in the way of fundamental reform, considering the present state of affairs in our intermediate educational world. Should, however, the advocates of this effective system become numerous among English teachers of middle schools, and should they co-operate in favour of this system, it will by degrees gain ground in middle schools. Mr. Swan then showed the arrangement of full lessons in his method as follows :

1. Greeting.
2. Incidents.
3. Lesson.
4. Conversation.
5. Grammar.
6. Phonetics.
7. Literature.
8. Morals.

If a teacher is skilful, he said, one hour will be enough to practice all these items, but in a case of the teacher who is slower, the lessons may be systematically divided into several hours. In this way, students will make great progress in two or three years ; and their linguistic knowledge will become steady and practical, in a way to which the present roundabout method of teaching can never attain. The professor called the attention of his pupils to the importance of occasionally beginning their lessons with the narration of some personal incidents, occurring to students on the previous day or on the way to school. This will not only interest them and give them fresh vigor to attend to their regular lessons, but also will serve to practise the chief conjugations and tenses. It will be well also to mark a few interesting paragraphs in newspapers and tell them in class-rooms in the five minutes before entering on the next lesson. Prof. Swan next wrote down on the board the names of the English alphabet in phonetics according to the request of one of the students.

The English Alphabet in Phonetics.

A	È : I	**J**	DJÈ : I	**S**	ÉS
B	Bɪɪ :	**K**	KÈ : I	**T**	Tɪɪ :
C	Sɪɪ :	**L**	È : ɛʟ	**U**	Yᴜᴜ :
D	Dɪɪ :	**M**	É : M	**V**	Vɪɪ :
E	Iɪ :	**N**	É : N	**W**	Dœɪ'ʟYᴜᴜ
F	EFF	**O**	☉ : ᴜ	**X**	EKS
G	DJII :	**P**	Pɪɪ	**Y**	WAA : I
H	È : ɪᴛᴄʜ	**Q**	KYUU :	**Z**	ZÉ : D
I	Aᴀɪ	**R**	Aᴀɛ(ʀ)		

He also explained the individual sounds of the alphabet, the vowels of which had already been illustrated by phonetics. He now turned to the teaching of complete sentences and taught the following order :

1. Verb. 2. Participle. 3. Actor.
4. Modification of the actor. 5. Article.

6. Thing acted upon.　7. Modification of the thing.

8. Article.　　　　9. Secondary thing.

10. Modification.　11. Article.　12. Preposition.

(This is for a simple sentence: to it will be added the conjunction and the second part of the sentence, if it be a compound sentence.)

The foregoing order was illustrated upon the sentence mentioned below; but is applicable to most sentences such as are used in the lessons on this method.

"The blacksmith takes a box of matches out of his pocket."

The following order was voted by the students.

1. takes	2. out	3. smith	4. black
5. the	6. box	7. a	8. matches
9. of	10. pocket	11. his	12. of

It is thus seen that there is truly a scientific order of teaching words in any sentence. If this order is taken, better results are obtained than if the right order is not considered.

2nd Hour.

OBJECTIVE AND SUBJECTIVE LANGUAGES.

The professor advised the students that the subjective language should be taught along with the objective language, and that they should try to choose appropriate subjective sentences for class use. He set an ingenious example of teaching subjective sentences side by side with a lesson on sequences of actions (objective sentences), so that the two lessons are carried on at the same time.

OBJECTIVE AND SUBJECTIVE.

LESSON XV.

I.—Sequences of Actions—Objective.

FISHING.

Scene : a bed room, then the bank of a river.

Verbs.	Complete Sentences.
gets up	A fisherman gets up early in the morning.
takes	He takes his fishing tackle.
comes out	He comes out of his house.
goes down	He goes down to the river.
chooses	He chooses a good place to fish.
sets down	He sets down his fishing tackle on the edge of the river.
put together	He puts his fishing rod together.
adjust	He adjusts the line.
fastens	He fastens the hook to the line.
baits	He baits the hook with a worm (or a fly).
throws	He casts his line.
wasts	He waits patiently.
has	He has a bite.
lands	He lands a fish.
unhooks	He unhooks the fish.
put	He put the fish into his basket.

II.—Teachers and Pupils' Sentences—Subjective.

There are a few difficulties in this lesson, but they are
so small they are hardly worth while speaking about.
I will prompt you. I will whisper to you.
Don't whisper; it's not polite in good society.
Anyone might think you were saying something bad.
If you have secrets, tell them some other time.

63

I have no secrets from you.
Somebody whispered to you, didn't they ?—No.
Answer me frankly.
Did anyone whisper to you ?—No !
Will you swear ? On your honour ?
Well, I believe you.
You are difficult to convince.

The order in teaching the sentences of the subjective language is somewhat similar to that for the objective language, but the principal word is not always the verb. For instance, in such subjective sentences as " I have a secret," or " It is difficult,"—" secret " and " difficult " are the important words. In teaching these phrases, the first requisite is to create the corresponding feeling in the mind or heart of the pupils. Then (usually after giving the Japanese translation) a sentence is to be built up around the important word, searching for clear instances of its true use, and repeating it distinctly with correct accents. If possible, three or four examples of a subjective word should be given, to bring out the full force of its meaning. For instance, in the explanation of such a phrase as " hardly worth while," the following three examples may be found suitable :

It is hardly worth while to catch a certain train.
It is hardly worth while to pay so much money.
It is hardly worth while to send a telegram.

3rd Hour.
READING.

From " Flashes from the Far East." From several chapters. About 10 pages. Reading and pronunciation.

With the lesson on reading, came the conclusion of the lectures on the Psychological Method of studying English. The professor then wished everyone pleasure and profit in endeavouring to adopt the principles of the method. It is not absolutely necessary, he said, to adopt all the exact details at once, yet the following three principles could be usefully employed by all teachers of English:

1. Give clear mental pictures. And in any lesson of objective fact, endeavour not to change the scene too frequently. Keep the same scene.
2. In teaching the subjective language or idioms of thought and emotion, explain literally first and then idiomatically, always giving at least three examples. In this case, change the picture often, giving striking instances.
3. In giving the grammar lessons, use examples which apply directly to the student's life or action, either in the class or in his home life, and never take abstract examples to illustrate grammatical rules.

If in addition to these three principles, scientifically constructed text-books are used and the teaching of phonetics is given, the mastery of the English language can be made a fairly easy and a really pleasurable task.

The Summer School then broke up with many expressions of gratitude on the part of the students for the varied lessons they had received.

End.

大賣捌所

全 全

神田區裏神保町　　神田區表神保町

三省堂　――　上田屋　　中西屋

日本橋區通三丁目　丸善書店

複製不許

印刷所　株式會社東京築地活版製造所　東京市京橋區築地二丁目十七番地

發行所　國民英學會出版局　東京市神田區錦町三丁目十九番地

印刷者　難波木曾治　東京市神田區錦町三丁目十九番地

發行者　磯邊彌一郎　東京市麴町區三番町八十四番地

著作者　安藤貫一

著作者　英國人　ハワード・スワン

明治三十五年十月廿三日發行

明治三十五年十月二十日印刷

スワン氏英語敎授法

明治三十七年夏期金沢英語講習会筆記

Résumé of Lectures Given at the Summer School of English.

RÉSUMÉ
OF
LECTURES

GIVEN AT THE

SUMMER SCHOOL OF ENGLISH

(1904)

明治三十七年夏期

金澤英語講習會筆記

全

SANSEIDO.

RÉSUMÉ

OF

LECTURES

GIVEN AT THE

SUMMER SCHOOL OF ENGLISH
(1904)

BY

PROF. GAUNTLETT,
PROF. McKENZIE,
PROF. ELLIOTT,

WRITTEN AND ARRANGED

BY

K. ANDO.

TOKYO:
SANSEIDO.

PREFACE.

The contents of the present volume were originally intended for the perusal of my fellow-teachers in the Uyeda Middle School. But finding that many of the lectures were not only suggestive to the generality of teachers of English, but also practically helpful to all those studying the language, I felt inclined to prepare my copy for the public. The advice of a few friends to the same effect, confirmed me in this idea, and the result is the present publication. The lectures were written from day to day in haste, and sufficient time was not allowable for arranging them properly. But the copy having been carefully revised by the three professors, I have pleasure in assuring the readers that they have in hand a reliable report of the lectures delivered.

Kan-ichi Andō.

Tokyo, August, 1904.

INTRODUCTION.

The Educational Department has made it a rule of recent years to open Summer Schools for the benefit of those engaged in the work of education in middle schools, normal schools and higher girls' schools. It is really an excellent idea of the Authorities to afford the teachers a chance, once a year, of rubbing up on their specialities. True, the term of the schools is very limited ; but then with a large degree of serious attention, the teachers are able to glean useful fragments of knowledge, together with valuable suggestions. If the advantage they derive therefrom can be said to influence general education for the better, even indirectly, it is difficult to exaggerate the importance of the schools in question. This is all the more true, when we take into consideration the utilisation of a greater part of the summer vacation, which might otherwise be squandered, for the most part, in idle pursuits.

In the summer of the year before last, Prof. Swan delivered a series of lectures on the Psychological Method of Teaching English, in Tokyo, to more than one hundred teachers. His lectures, with all his inadaptable suggestions and high-flying remarks, did much to open the eyes of the teachers present to the necessity of systematic instruction in the language, and caused them to introduce a certain number of improvements into their way of teaching. Encouraged by this example, many looked for similar help again

2   INTRODUCTION.

last year, but for some reason unknown to them, there
was to their great disappointment, no summer school
opened for lectures on the English language.

Our hearty thanks are due to a few educationalists
in Kanazawa, whose joint exertion in our behalf is
said to have had much to do with the Teachers' Summer School opened there this year. The number of
those in attendance was found to be smaller than
that at the similar school opened in Tokyo two years
ago—there being but sixty-nine in all. They were
nevertheless eager students of English, faithful in
their work, who came to that comparatively out - of -
the - way place from every direction,—some from
Formosa, some from Loochoo, and some from the
Hokkaido. As long as there remain such enthusiastic
teachers of English in Japan, the prospect of English
education in this country will never be so hopeless
as some imagine.

We were officially directed to arrive at Kanazawa on
the 24th of July and to apply to the Fourth High
School, in which the said summer school was to be
opened, for necessary items of information. Here we
were informed among other things that we were to
appear there precisely at seven next morning. The
majority of us actually did as were directed, though
a few failed to put in an appearance by the given
time. The result was that a quarter past seven passed
without anything happening; half past seven, and still
nothing; eight, still nothing,—and all this while we
were left to ourselves in the waiting-room, some smok-
ing, some looking at the time-table, and some grum-
bling. It was ten minutes past eight when we were

finally ushered into the lecture hall and took our respective seats.

MR. YOSHIMURA'S ADDRESS.

We had scarcely taken our seats before an elderly gentleman with a smiling face, and dressed in European costume, appeared on the platform, and introduced himself as Torataro Yoshimura, Director of the Fourth High School. I was not a little surprised to see his face; it was not strange to me. I remember that it was in April this year that a stranger accompanied by the head of the Uyeda Middle School, to which I belong, entered the Fifth Year Class without previous announcement, and watched my teaching for one whole hour, making me feel it hard to retain my composure. He was no other than Mr. Yoshimura now standing before us!

Introducing us to the three lecturers, ex-Prof. McKenzie of the Fourth High School, Prof. Gauntlett of Okayama High School, and Prof. Elliott of Hiroshima Higher Normal School, he explained how the present summer school had come to be opened in Kanazawa. "Mr. Hisata, head of the First Middle School here," he said, "left no pains unspared in bringing about the opening of a summer school here this year. Last summer, he and some thirty other English teachers, including myself, advised the Authorities to the same effect, but it was in vain, on account of the fact that the latter had already made

4   MR. YOSHIMURA'S ADDRESS.

public the programme of lectures on certain branches
of learning. We asked Mr. McKenzie and Mr.
Gauntlett, therefore, to give private lectures on
English in this place, and exchanged our opinions on
methods of teaching the language. And the theories
stated were practically tested in teaching a number
of students of one of the middle schools, assembled
for the purpose."

Then referring to the inadequate knowledge of
English possessed by the average student of middle
schools, he said: Ever since the Fifth Year of Meiji,
down to the present, English has occupied an important part in the middle school curriculum. But
the student's knowledge is as imperfect as ever,
notwithstanding the considerable amount of time
which is set apart for the teaching of the language.
This is chiefly ascribable to imperfect methods of
teaching. It is of urgent necessity that those concerned should meet and try to find out some way by
means of which they can teach with less effort and
with more effect. Most students are in the habit of
handling difficult books, considering 'Yakudoku'
(translation) to be the sole aim of language study.
For instance, until quite recently, it was usually
found that the majority of candidates for this school
gave a long list of hard books they had superficially
skimmed over. In reality, there were unable to understand even the easier language of the 'Readers'
quite correctly. Though their notion of language
study has improved of late to a certain extent, they
still have a tendency to attach too much importance
to translation to the neglect of more useful branches

MR. YOSHIMURA'S ADDRESS.   5

—speaking and writing. We must first of all break
them entirely of this bad habit, and then turn their
attention to the acqisition of a practical knowledge
of English. To attain that end, text-books are required to be compiled in such a manner as to answer
the purpose. In the meantime, books of familiar
English should be taught conscientiously in middle
schools, the students being required to review them
as often as possible. They can thus master words
and phrases of daily use which, with practice, can
be used with exactness in speaking or in writing."

He concluded his address by reminding the audience
of the absolute necessity of English in the educational
institutions of intermediate grade, and declaring that
as civilization progressed, instruction in this language
would grow more and more important. "The Japan-
Russia War," he said, "will have a far-reaching influence over our education, and at the same time, the
necessity of English instruction will be enhanced."

He then gave the reason why the meeting was not
opened at seven. "On account of the fact that a few
gentlemen failed to come in season, the necessary
arrangements could not be made until a little after
eight. Hence the delay. But from to-morrow lectures
by the professors will be begun exactly at eight ; so
I hope you will be punctual."

His address, which was made in Japanese, occupied
some fifteen minutes.

CHAPTER. I.

INTRODUCTORY ADDRESS, BY PROF. McKENZIE.

Prof. McKenzie, a gentleman of middle stature, with a fine moustache, addressing the audience in his sonorous English, alluded first to the reason which caused the time-table to be issued so very late. "We three teachers live in cities distant from one another," he said, "and each having had his own work to do from the end of April, when the arrangements for the school were made, down to the beginning of July, we had no opportunity of meeting together to settle upon and arrange the subjects of our lectures. Of course we corresponded on the subject, but this was not sufficient to enable us to decide matters with entire satisfaction. It was only a few days ago that we met and consulted in regard to the making of the time-table. This being the case, we have had no time to prepare a sufficiently comprehensive programme. A question box, however, will be provided to help make up for the incompleteness of the programme. Any questions you may wish to ask may be put into the box, and they will be considered and answered to the best of our ability."

He then entered on his assigned topic by saying that he believed it was Macaulay who had made the assertion that one of adult age could never learn to speak a foreign language perfectly. In learning a foriegn language, children have a great advantage. A child born in a foriegn land or coming to it when two or three years old, will learn to speak and understand the language of that land as readily as it does its mother tongue. He had been in Japan more than sixteen years, and yet it was hard for him to speak Japanese with correctness and fluency. On the other hand his children, who were born in Japan, could express themselves tolerably well in Japanese without any special effort. In their case the language had "soaked in,"— they were environed by its atmosphere, and by constant imitation they mastered the common idioms and the manner of uttering them. These are the advantages children have over us grown-up people, who endeavor to study a foreign language by means very different from those used by the children.

Every language has its own idioms and figures. And each differs more or less widely from the others in the way of expressing thought. The languages of the nations develop through channels different from one another; though the process of the growth of thought is found to be much the same all the world over. A comparative study of the proverbs of various nations would show that there are many corresponding to one another in thought. It is the mode of expressing ideas that differs. So when one attempts the study of a foreign language, he must not only learn new sounds and words and construction of sentences, but must also learn the new idioms and figures of speech. This, however, would not be so difficult, were it not for the fact that there are so many exceptions to rules, so many irregularities in all languages. No language is perfect and no grammar is complete. Greek, which is considered the most perfect language that ever existed, had its various dialects and other irregularities, rendering it difficult for the student to master it. No wonder, then, that English, derived as it is from so many sources, has numerous irregularities. To take a single example, the plurals of English nouns are formed after the fashion of Saxon, French, Greek, Latin and Hebrew plurals. So the rule of adding "s" or "es" to the singular of nouns to form the plural, is not by any means a complete rule for making plurals. Many other similar examples might be given. Again, English has a variety of sounds which, though familiar to Englishmen and Americans, are difficult for the Japanese to distinguish. To give an example, the letter "a" has as many as six sounds, but we Englishmen find no difficulty whatever in showing these differences with accuracy. The same, however, cannot be hoped from foreigners studying the language. And it is only by dint of constant practice that they can measurably make the necessary distinctions. Irregularities in English spelling form another great difficulty for the student. In studying foreign languages the irregularities and exceptions make us impatient. But this does no good. We should recognize the fact that they are inevitable. Language is not made ; it grows. It is not built up, like a house, according to fixed measurements, but grows up irregularly, like a tree. A student can never attain proficiency in it as long as he treats it as an exact science. He must make allowances for the numerous irregularities. A thorough scholar of Greek, Latin and other languages in America was once asked how he came to know these languages so perfectly. "By plodding," was his brief reply. Students of English would do well to remember the significance contained in his simple yet sensible reply. Only by "plodding" can you acquire a thorough knowledge of English. The English teacher in middle schools and, I presume, in normal schools as well, has one of the most important positions of all in the teaching of English. It is in these schools that the foundation of a knowledge of English is laid. Hence the importance of the work. To investigate effective methods of teaching English, is a heavy duty laid upon the teachers of that language in such schools. "My two friends," he concluded, "have long been in Japan, and have a wide experience in language teaching, and they are well qualified to give you a great many practical suggestions along this line."

PROFESSOR GAUNTLETT'S LECTURES.

CHAPTER II.

INTRODUCTORY TO PHONETICS.

Prof. Gauntlett is an English gentleman, short, but well built, with an intelligent face and active manners. He is said to have many talents, and belongs to that class of men who put their hands to everything they take an interest in, and come off well. He has an acquaintance with Latin and Greek, is an admirable musician, a specialist in Phonetics, a successful practitioner of Hypnotism, an initiator of the newest shorthand, a philologist, and a good cyclist.

The following is a general outline of his lecture, which he delivered in rare good English.

Phonetics is an important subject for one studying foreign languages, especially in the case of Japanese teachers.

Dr. Sweet gives in his book on Phonetics the degrees of difference in pronunciation existing in several languages. To Englishmen, it is difficult to speak French, German, or Spanish with ease: much more so for Japanese studying English, which is entirely different from their tongue. "I always find," he said, "on the occasion of the entrance examination at our school, the Okayama High School, that the ability to understand and speak English differs greatly among the candidates. Some few can understand and speak English pretty well, but most of them

PROF. GAUNTLETT'S LECTURES. 11

have a very limited knowledge in that line; and their
pronunciation is generally indistinct and full of errors.
That pronunciation is very difficult to acquire, holds
true in every case of people learning a foreign language. I was born in Wales and learned to speak
its language a little. Now the language of Wales is
very different from English, and it is no easy matter
for the Welsh to learn English, its pronunciation
and manner of expression being hard for Welshmen
to master. Although a language may have a great
number of dialects, these will gradually diminish in
number as communication and commerce increase,
because by means of intercommunication, one dialect
influences another and becomes more like it, until
they are centred in one."

People study foreign languages for different purposes, some for practical uses, such as trade, commerce, travelling, etc., others for acquiring a knowledge of the sciences through their medium. And
again, some scholars study dead languages, such as
Greek and Latin, for the purpose of translating ancient documents and inscriptions. But to study a
foreign language in order to read books only, is of
minor importance. To make a practical study of a
language, one has ever to pay special attention to
its pronunciation; for if it be once acquired wrongly,
it is hard to correct it. Hence the necessity of
carefully teaching students the exact pronunciation
from the outset. But there are in most languages,
peculiar sounds which can hardly be learned simply
by imitation. For instance, Englishmen find difficulty
in pronouncing the French words "du vin," the

PROF. GAUNTLETT'S LECTURES.

German word "buch" and the Welsh word "llaw." The latter contains an "l mute," whereas Englishmen often make the mistake of substituting "thl," and saying "thlaw." Mr. Gauntlett can pronounce all Persian letters except ڨ and ع (Qaf and Ghain), and the reason he cannot pronounce these is that he has had no phonetic analysis of them.

He then proceeded to the subject of Phonetics, as a faithful guide in attaining right pronunciation; and recommended us to study a book on Japanese Phonetics written by Mr. Okakura, preparatory to taking up the study of English Phonetics, because in doing so, one has the advantage of thus being prepared for the easier investigation of the sounds of English letters. He compared the vocal organs to a reed organ. As an organ is made to produce musical tones by the wind from bellows through a reed, so the vocal organs are made to sound by causing the breath from the lungs to pass through a reed, and then out by the mouth. And as proper sounds do not come out of an organ when its bellows, pipes, and keys are out of order, so right sounds are not produced by the vocal organs when the lungs are very weak and the tongue, teeth, and lips are not in proper positions to give the right sounds. To be a good organ-builder, one must know the construction and mechanism of organs; for a similar reason, one must know the proper position of the vocal organs in order to be able to utter the particular sounds of letters, and also constantly to exercise pronunciation, or modifications of all sounds. The lungs have much to do with distinct pronunciation, so it is well for students of English to keep them in sound condition by means of deep breathing exercises. All these things are treated of in Phonetics. He said that Phonetics was the grammar of pronunciation; difficult, but useful; and grammar was a subject, he said with a smile, that he hated while at school. Grammar, which simply classes and gives laws, should not be studied mechanically by itself, but be attended by constant exercise in speaking and writing, for grammar does not *make* language, but is simply a result of it. In Phonetics, likewise, practice in pronunciation should be made from time to time. He said that the sounds " f " and " th " were hard for foreigners to distinguish; so he often writes on the blackboards serveral words containing these letters, and makes his pupils repeat them over and over again in a loud voice. Sometimes he stands behind the class and reads some of them, to see if they are able to distinguish them. Example of Words Containing " f " and " th "

Flow   Throw
Breath passing out of   Strong teeth sound pro-
 the mouth, between   nounced rather sudden-
 the upper teeth and   ly, with the tongue
 the lower lip.   between the teeth.

He added that these two sounds are often mispronounced by young English or American children.

He then called our attention to the " tune," or inflection of voice which every language has, the imitation of which is very useful in language study.

14   PROF. GAUNTLETT'S LECTURES.

"When I was in Shanghai," he said, "I was one day asked by a Chinese to pronounce the word 'ping ting,' the Chinese for *soldier*, and I did it with an English accent, that is, with a falling inflection; but the Chinaman told me that it must be pronounced in a high tone, quite different from anything in English." Then he mentioned the language-tunes characteristic to French, and German, the former nasal and quick, the latter rather emphatic and deliberate. There is a student in the 1st class of his school who imitates, in conversation, not only his inflection, but his every gesture, and by dint of exertion, he has made much improvement in English conversation. Welsh has commonly much inflection of voice; French has in most cases a rising inflection at the end of sentences. To show by diagrams:

French :   Comment vous portez-vous ?

Welsh :   Sut yr ydych i chwi heddyw ?

English :   How do you do ?

Germans and Frenchmen use very many gestures when talking; for instance a Frenchman, rather than say, "Je ne sais pas," (I don't know), would only shrug his shoulders and turn up the palms of his hands.

He then made reference to English dictionaries in vogue, saying that their respective marks for pronunciation are more or less different and that this was very puzzling for Japanese students of English. For instance, "a" in some dictionaries represents ェ₄ -, in others, ア - : in "fert*i*le" the letter *i* may be ィ or ア ィ. "Vase" has five pronunciations. "Been"

PROF. GAUNTLETT'S LECTURES. 15

has two pronunciations, "bēn," and "bĭn". "Haunt" is pronounced in England "hawnt," and in America "hänt." The best dictionaries are the "Standard," the "Century," "Webster," and the "Imperial." The pronunciation authorized by these dictionaries are understood anywhere in England, America, Australia, and India. "Stick to the pronunciation you choose so long as it is recognized, and do not trouble yourselves much in the matter of differences."

Notes—

1. A Frenchman can often tell an Englishman by his pronunciation of "p."
2. In English the lips and vocal organs are moved more than in Japanese.
3. Two pronunciations of "was"—
    (*a*) "woz" (in formal speaking or when emphasized).
    (*b*) "wz" (in ordinary speaking).

CHAPTER III.

PHONETICS.

The professor drew the following diagram on the blackboard, to begin with:

1. upper lip
2. lower lip
3. teeth
4. hard palate
5. uvula (soft palate)
6. throat
7. epiglottis (a kind of valve which opens and shuts)
8. nasal passage
9. vocal chord (like a reed: consisting of two membranes

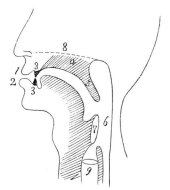

which shut and open like the following diagrams

Explanations followed, and the sounds of the English letters were classed as follows:
1. Lip—labial as, p, b, m, wh, w.
2. Teeth—dental as, t, d, th, *th*.
3. Palate—palatal as, sh, zh, s, z.
4. Nose—nasal as, m, n, ng.
5. Throat—guttural as, k, g, h.

He told us that the lungs, which are like the bellows of an organ, should be exercised by taking deep breaths and then expelling the air slowly. This exercise is a great help in making one a clear speaker.

He then explained the various shapes of vocal chord when speaking:

Blowing   h   Whispering   Voice

"wh" in "when, what, where, which," etc., is pronounced by the uneducated and even by some educated people, with "h" silent, but this usage is not to be recommended. "Wh" is pronounced something like the Japanese *kana* ふ, the difference being that in the latter the lips are a trifle more rounded and compressed.

The lips may be said to resemble the "swell" cover in an organ, and are very important in pronunciation; but the sounds of lip letters are not difficult. Englishmen, Germans, and Frenchmen move their lips more emphatically than the Japanese. French is a nasal language and its final "on, an, in" are particularly nasal. Americans generally speak English more nasally than Englishmen.

All the letters are divisible into two kinds:

1. Explodents, (the sounds sudden, the breath stopped) as, p, b, t, d, k, g.

2. Continuants, (all others.)

PROF. GAUNTLETT'S LECTURES.

All letters are divided into two classes, mutes (or surds) and sonants. Such letters as f, s, h, etc., are mutes, while all the vowels and the "voiced" consonants are sonants. In the sound of 人 (hito) the vowel "i" is made almost mute. Japanese students are likewise apt to make "i" silent in such English words as "Capital," "City," or they whisper the vowel, whereas Englishmen pronounce it clearly.

CHAPTER IV.

PHONETICS.

Mr. Gauntlett first wrote on the blackboard the following classification of English sounds, in a clear bold hand :

Stopped				Continuants				
		Sibilants		nasal				
Labials P b			} F v {	m				Wh w
Dentals T d		S z	} Th th {	n	l	ray		y
Palatals	Sh zh							
Gutturals K g				ng			H	

(In the foregoing table the capital letters are intended for mutes ; the others for sonants)

He then explained the positions and motions of the sounds peculiar to each letter, the hard ones by means of diagrams. Below are given some of the difficult sounds which he clearly explained.

" P "   " It is strange," he said, " that the exact sound of " p " is not often heard in Japanese. Englishmen and Americans pronounce the letter with sudden separation of the lips, the sound stopping immediately, whereas Japanese people often prolong the sound, so that in listening to them pronouncing such a word as " top," they often seem to say " topf." The reason is

	partly ascribable to their not opening the mouth quite as wide as foreigners do.
"Wh"	is pronounced by blowing between the lips, somewhat as when whistling.
"W"	is a very short ŭ, as in the words *wolf* (ŭ-ūlf), *weak* (ŭ-ēk).
"T"	English "T" is sharper than Japanese "T" in the *gojūin*, as Italian is sharper than English, as in "*t*ra." Europeans often say they cannot distinguish English *tr* from *ch*, which latter is t + sh. The sound of T is produced by touching the tip of the tongue to the roof of the mouth just above the teeth, and suddenly taking it away, as if in the diagram :

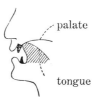

"F" "v"	These two sounds do not exist in Japanese, and ㋪, which is often used in its place, is entirely different from either of them. The upper teeth are placed on the lower lip and the breath is blown between, as in the diagram. *The upper lip is never used*, so even if a man lost it by an accident, he could pronounce these two letters plainly.

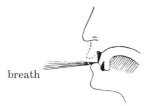

When Mr. Gauntlett taught in a middle school in Tokyo some years ago, he found it very hard to tell the boys in the first year class how to pronounce this sound. As he made the strange sound, some of them smiled, and as they did so, they accidentally placed their mouths in the right position for the sound. And he often recommended the position of the mouth in smiling, in teaching the sound of "F" and "V." The audience could not help laughing, not at the exercise of the sound, but at this comical yet practical suggestion.

"Th" In pronouncing the letters no hissing sound is caused as in "s," but simply the sound of blowing :

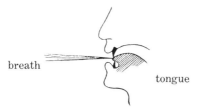

As shown in the diagram given above, the

PROF. GAUNTLETT'S LECTURES.

end of the tongue is placed just between the teeth, and the breath escapes between the very slight aperture between the upper teeth and the tongue. If the teeth were closed, while saying "th" we should almost bite off the end of the tongue. This is the sensation we experience when pronouncing "Th." The professor advised us to drill ourselves in the pronunciation of "Th" and "s" by contrasting such words, as :

think - sink.　thank - sank.
bath - brass.

"N"　　Every Japanese word is said by foreigners to end in a vowel, excepting "ン" which has a vowel-like sound. The Japanese represent English "n" by "ン," but it is a mistake. When the letter precedes a vowel, its sound corresponds to Japanese "ナ ニ ヌ ネ ノ," and at the end of a word, it has precisely the same sound, as if a slight "u" were heard after it, as in "nation," which might be represented in *Kana* by ネイショヌ." We often notice that such a phrase "in an instant" as "is apt to be represented by *Kana*, as "in an instant."
イン アン インスタント
This is not right; if we must use *Kana* at all, (which should be avoided,) it should be written as "in‿an‿instant." We
イナ ニヌ スタヌト
notice that 山陽 of the Sanyo Railway, is

PROF. GAUNTLETT'S LECTURES. 23

written in Roman letters as "Sanyo, but we are rather puzzled how to read it, for we cannot tell whether it is "Sa-nyo" or "San-yo." If it is intended for the latter sound, it might be better to use the Sapanish *n̂* rather than *n*.

CHAPTER V.

PHONETICS.

Mr. Gauntlett's lecture treated of the sounds of letters, continued from the preceding day.

"L" In pronouncing this letter, the relation of the tongue to the roof of the mouth is not unlike that of "T," that is to say, the top of the tongue touches the gums; the only difference is that in the case of "L," the breath passes out by either one or both sides of the tongue, as:

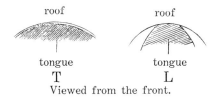

Viewed from the front.

As to the sound of "R," the tongue is curled back:

In some countries, "R" has a strong trill, as in Germany, Bohemia, Wales, Ireland,

and the north of England. In fact, some
Europeans often confuse the pronunciation of "train" and "chain." "R" has
a little trill before a vowel, as : "rat,"
"root" "right." But at the end of a
syllable or a word, it has practically
none.

Phoneticians disagree in their opinions a-
bout the sound of "R." Sweet and Soames
in England and Vietor in Germany are
of opinion that it is almost a vowel.
In England "R" preceded by a vowel
is practically silent as regards the trill,
as in "per," "sir," "cur" etc.; but in
America it has a slightly stronger sound.
In "iron" "R" has a vowel sound, but
in "ironical" it is a consonant. He has
now been fourteen years in Japan, and
yet his experience as a teacher has not
enabled him to give clear distinction
between "R" and "L" to Japanese
students. In teaching them to distinguish
"l" from "r" in the lips of Englishmen,
it may be observed that "L" contains
something of the sound of "u" at the
end of it, while "R" is sounded near the
throat. Practice should be made in
such words, as "clear" "creep, "claim"
"crape" to learn the distinction between
the two letters well. In pronouncing
"T" the tongue separates itself from
the upper palate rather suddenly ; in the

PROF. GAUNTLETT'S LECTURES.

case of "L" the force of separation is as quick, but as the tongue is already open at the sides, this separation is less distinctly heard. With "R" the case is quite different, as it has a "rolling back" motion of the tongue. Pronunciation of the following syllables soon manifests the difference.

la   ra   li   ri   lu   ru

le   re   lo   ro

"Sh" "S" Both sounds are hard for Japanese students to distinguish when they come before a vowel, especially *e*, as : "sea," and "she." "Sh" is sounded by touching the point of the blade of the tongue to the gums, like in Japanese " ス " and "S" by touching the blade itself, with teeth closed a little and the lips slightly projecting. In the sound of the former letter, therefore, the vocal organs are in a slightly less constrained position than in the latter. The distinction is easily learned by pronouncing " so "—" show," " saw "—" shaw " " see "—" she," " Sark " —" shark," " say "—" shay."

"zh" (as in confusion) Care must be taken to distinguish " zh " (continuant, and so no break of voice) from " J " which is a stopped sound. In English " zh " never come at the beginning of a word.

Note. J = d + zh.

PROF. GAUNTLETT'S LECTURES.   27

"Ng"   This is pronounced by making the breath
           pass through the nose while placing the
           tongue in the *K* position. It is always
           final to a syllable as in "Ki*ng*."
"K" "G"   (much stronger than Japanese " ク " and
           " グ ") "G" is never pronounced like " ガ "
           in the Tokyo dialect.
"H"   (throat letter, true guttural) It corresponds
           nearly to Japanese " ハ " " ヘ " " ホ," when
           joined to vowels. The difference between
           h and " ヒ " " フ " is that while " ヒ " and
           " フ " are sounded by the mouth, *h* is
           sounded in the throat. "H" is always
           sounded in America, but in England un-
           educated, and some educated people omit it,
           as in w*h*en," "w*h*ere," "w*h*at." Perhaps
           this is owing to the influence of European
           languages, as Italian and French, which
           have silent "H." Englishmen of the lower
           classes often add "H" before a word
           begun with a vowel.   In illustration of
           this, the professor related an amusing
           story. Once when he was in Ceylon, he
           took a carriage to a certain place. Seeing
           an English soldier sitting besides him, he
           said; "What regiment do you belong to?"
           "The Light Infantry," he replied. But
           the noise of the carriage prevented the
           professor from catching the words dis-
           tinctly. On inquiring a second time, the
           soldier cried in a loud voice, "*The Light
           Hinfantry!*"

28   PROF. GAUNTLETT'S LECTURES.

In response to a few questions put in the " Question
Box," the lecturer gave satisfactory explanations. The
important ones are as follows:—

Ques.   " What is the distinction between short i
             (as in th*i*nk) and short y (as in *York*)? "
Ans.   " *Y* in *York* is shorter and more com-
             pressed than i in th*i*nk."
Ques.   " How to read figures? "
Ans.   This is very easy; we only divide figures
             at every hundredth part and read using
             " and " after the word hundred, as :

      1 4 1,   3 4 5,   2 7 7,   5 4 1.
      billion   million   thousand

read: One hundred and forty-one billion three
             hundred and forty-five million two hundred
             and seventy-seven thousand five hundred
             and forty-one.

CHAPTER VI.

PHONETICS.

Table of vowel Sounds.

Lips	Back of Mouth		Middle of Mouth		Front.	
	Round		Round		Round	
open	caw ⏋ ⷆ	ah ᵣ ⊣				
	not ⊣					
Half open	So ⊣	ʳ such ⊣		(obscure) cur ⌋		set ⊣ ᵡ care ⌋ men ⌋ say
Close	food ⏋ put ⊣					feel ⏋ ⷆ fill ⊣

(Notes: ⏋ ⊣ ⌋ respectively indicate the height of the tongue, high, middle, or low, as:

The letters underlined are diphthongs.)

PROF. GAUNTLETT'S LECTURES.

"A" as in "*caw*" is rather similar to the Japanese オ - ; only it is a little stronger in sound, the tongue being further back.

"O" as in "*so*" is the sound of the two vowels オ - ウ combined, and no Englishman utters the sound without moving his lips ; but most of the Japanese students pronounce it オ - as if it were one vowel sound, whereas it is really a diphthong.

"U" as in "*put*" is very much like the Japanese ウ.

"Ah" is deeper, and uttered with the month more open than in ア.

"U" as in "*nut*" and "*such*" is pronounced by drawing the tongue slightly back and keeping it midway between the jaws.

"E" as in "*set*" and "*a*" as in "*care*" both resemble the Japanese エ, their difference being in the position of the tongue ; but to analize their sound is difficult even to many Englishmen.

"E" as in "*feel*" is something like the Japanese イ -, but is a little stronger.

The professor then gave instances of letters which cannot be separated in sound when they come together in different words. In this case they are to be pronounced as one sound, but stronger, as :

They set‿traps. They bought‿dogs.
Book‿case. Black‿glass.
The top‿place. The top‿book.

PROF. GAUNTLETT'S LECTURES.   31

They both_think so.   Bees_said.
Fish_show.   Some_men.
At noon_next Saturday. Frail_leather.
Rough_view.

But in the following cases, the sound must be separated, as :

Which church?   Which judge?

This proves that the old doctrine, that ch and j were
single consonants, was a fallacy.   Care must be taken
not to pronounce the former ch as if it were t, a
common mistake among the Japanese, who often read
"which church" as if it were "Whitchurch."

Again we must be equally careful not to combine
such sonants as follows :

Was sure. "S" in "was," in such a case, has the
sound of "zh," because "s" in "sure" has that of
"sh ;" but they cannot be pronounced without separat-
ing them, if we keep to "dictionary rules."   Here
"was" should be read "wzh."

"D"   in "and" is usually omitted when follow-
             ed by dental letters, unless spoken slowly,
             as in the instance given below :

An(d) no man......

When pronouncing "n" as in "button" and "didn't,"
do not forget that nasal passage the shuts and opens
between d and n, and that the *tongue does not move.*

When "l" is preceded by dental letters + an obscure
vowel, *the top of the tongue does not descend from the
upper palate*, but only the sides open, as : Kettle,
ladle.

"Th"   when followed by "s" is difficult to

pronounce distinctly ; !and such a word as "twelf*ths*" is hard even for an Englishman to pronounce clearly.

Here the professor reminded us of the easy pronunciation of English words compared with some other European languages, which have numerous peculiar sounds, which make it hard for foreigners to get the right pronunciation of their words. He could not properly pronounce the Polish name "Dantzig," until a Polish gentleman told him that it should be sounded "Dntzg." When there is more than one pronunciation to a word, take one and keep it. For instance, "either" or "neither" are differently pronounced. Englishmen often pronounce them "i'ther" and "ni'-ther," Americans "e'ther" and "ne'ther." Again, in England "dew" is often pronounced like "jew," while in America it is pronounced "du." In such cases, it is advisable, as was said before, to stick to one pronunciation so long as it is a recognized one. The following books on phonetics were recommended :

1. English and German Sounds :
    by Grandgent.
2. Primer of Spoken English : (the best for Japanese teachers)
    by Sweet.
3. Elements of Phonetics :
    by Vietor.
4. Primer of Phonetics :
    by Sweet.

CHAPTER VII.

WRITING.

Some forty little boys of the 1st year class of the two middle schools in Kanazawa were conducted into the lecture hall, where they were to be given lessons in writing. Prof. Gauntlett told the teacher-students that it wås impossible in such a limited time to explain everything to be observed in this particular art. He was only going to give a few useful suggestions on the forms of the letters. He then told the boys, in good Japanese, to open their copy-books at page 8 and write. By the way, the copy-books they used were the ones he himself wrote and had much originality in them. He went round the room and gave several valuable suggestions to the boys, showing the relative length and thickness of letters, by writing specimens on the blackboard. For instance, he stated that the main lines of all letters must be parallel, and that the widths between them should be invariably like the marks on a scale, etc. as :

(good)   (wrong)   (wrong)

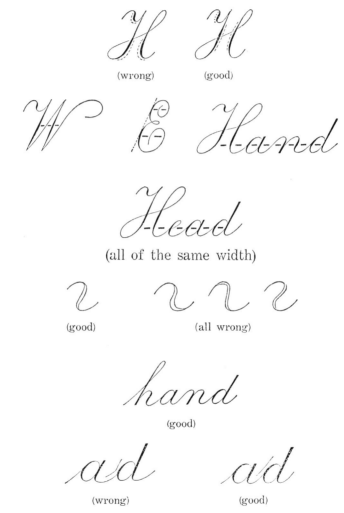

Addressing the teachers' class he said: "I am now preparing a new series of copy-books which I mean to get published by the Sanseido. There are two styles of vertical writing, one having thick and thin lines, and the other one thickness. I don't know which style you prefer. In a day or two I shall write a specimen in each style and ask you to give your opinion of them."

CHAPTER VIII.

WRITING.

The professor made the boys (1st year class) open their copy-books at a page on which was capital E. As usual, he went round the class, and gave various practical suggestions on the forms of letters. The reason he chose E was that it was more difficult to write than most letters. E is of the same height as the small letters, l, h etc.

Elephant

The lower part of E is larger than the upper, as:

The centre loop is a little above the true centre; the same rule applies in the case of many of the Roman Capital letters;

In rapid handwriting even words are often connected, as:

PROF. GAUNTLETT'S LECTURES.

You had better go to-day.

Italians often write with disjointed letters, so that it is hard at first for Englishmen to read them, as :

Nessun maggior dolore ____

The form *m* is a more favorite modern style

of wrting than *M.* It is better not to take the pen off the paper in writing the capitals. For this reason, the "Spencerian" copy-books, with all their originality, are not to be recommended. A point to be observed in writing the small letter "r."

right angle   obtuse angle   acute angle

best.   not so good.   bad.

Care must be taken in distinguishing the capital

M from *W* for many Japanese write it

38 PROF. GAUNTLETT'S LECTURES.

something like *M̸̸*.

The capital P must always rest on the line, as:

P P G J Y Z

To write *Please* like *please*

looks as bad as writing 東 like 軟

The capitals "G J Y Z" may go below the line.

CHAPTER IX.

PENMANSHIP.

It is to be regretted that the students of English at large do not pay so much attention to their handwriting as they should. In Europe and America, great importance is attached to the art, children being carefully trained in the use of the pen. As an illustration of this, the professor related an account of his own school days during which he underwent strict training in penmanship. If any one of the pupils wrote an illegible letter or letters, he was made to write it again and again until he could write it properly. In commercial schools in England and America, the students are particularly required to be very attentive to their handwriting, and they have to practise writing without resting their hands or arms on the desks, in this manner:

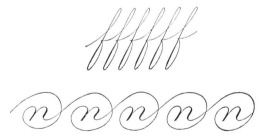

With regard to training, many things should be observed. It is important to practise moving the fingers and wrist freely; but in the case of young beginners, it is advisable that they should *draw* rather than write, in other words, they should learn to *form* the letters with a slow and careful movement of the pen. This is very tiring, but it should be done in order to lay the foundation of a good, clear form. A very, perhaps the most important point to be observed in writing, is regularity. The English letters, like those of any other European languages, are regular in their forms, whether it be in point of thickness, height, parallelism, and space between each line, as:

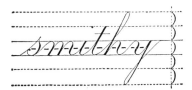

The professor then emphatically asserted that the principle of regularity applies to the letters of almost all languages, and gave a few examples in support of his assertions:

اسست   پیر   پدر   (Persian letters.)

ıı (n), ıı̆ (u), ıı (m), ıı (e)   (German.)

n (p), m (t), b, ъ   (Russian.)

He does not know, he said, much about the Chinese characters, but still this principle applies, he believes, to them also. To give an example, it is certainly not

PROF. GAUNTLETT'S LECTURES. 41

proper to write the character 書 thus: 書 or 書

The Spencerian style seems to be much in vogue in this country, as it used to be in America. But this style is not to be recommended, on account of the lack of distinctness and too great slope which prevails in the copy-books in question. In England, vertical and round styles are preferred.

Then he advised us to train students practically in writing, in their lessons in composition and dictation. If they are left to follow their own careless habits they will never improve in this art, whereas if they are continually warned and prompted, they will soon learn to write well. That students should write clearly and neatly is not only their own gain, but is an advantage to the teacher, for he can save much time in correcting well-written papers. For the same reason, Mr. Gauntlett is very particular in his way of giving lessons in composition or dictation. He continually tells his pupils to observe in writing compositions the following points :

1. To write " *Composition* " at the top of paper.
2. To write the date and the class they belong to, on the left, and their name on the right.
3. To write on alternate lines.
4. To leave a margin an inch wide on the left of the paper for critical marks and correction.

42   PROF. GAUNTLETT'S LECTURES.

SPECIMEN.

COMPOSITION.

Aug. 9th, 1904.   Class V.   *J. Smith*

One day, when I was in London,
I saw a man.....................

He then gave the following list of common mistakes made by Japanese students in writing, accompanied by useful suggestions :

1. *the* (wrong). *the, the* (right).

2. *The* (common among Japanese students, but not customary).

The (Englishmen's usual way of writing).

3. *Line* (wrong). *Line, Line,* (right).

4. *Queen* (wrong). *Queen* (right).

5. *don't* (not quite right). The form of

is final or sometimes medial, but not initial.

PROF. GAUNTLETT'S LECTURES. 43

6. *n (u)* *f (s)* (Almost obsolete.)

7. *Jn* (wrong). *Jn* (right).

8. *Sit* (wrong). *sit* (right).

9. *City* (wrong)

   city (right).

   } In the middle of a phrase.

10. *Ear, Eve* (both incorrect).

    Ear, Eve (right).

11. *a* (wrong). It is so written when one holds a penholder pointing outward.

    a (right).

12. *G* (wrong). *G G* (right).

Various forms of letters.

1. *Angular*

2. *Upright Round*

3. *Civil Service*

4. **ELEVATION**

5. *Line*

Specimens of flourishes and early illuminated initials were also given.

CHAPTER X.

PREPOSITIONS.

One of the most difficult points in the study of English is the use of prepositions. There is more or less similarity among the European languages so far the question of prepositions is concerned. Englishmen or Americans studying French or German do not find great difficulty in mastering them. In French "à" and "en" respectively correspond to the English prepositions "at" and "in," and the students rarely make any serious mistakes in their use. But the case is entirely different with Japanese students studying English. Besides the different manner of speaking and thinking, they have to surmount the difficulty of acquiring the proper use of the English prepositions, which are quite foreign to their own language. The worst of it is, they can hardly get any grammar which fully illustrates all the delicate shades of meanings involved in the English prepositions. Nor can they get a foreign teacher who is able to trace them back to their origin and give so practical an explanation as to help them out of the difficulty. For the same reason, the Japanese *te, ni, o, ha*, which are called "Postpositions" by some grammarians, are equally hard for foreigners to learn; and the professor told us he had himself studied them a long time, but without success. In many languages, prepositions are used very little, especially in the case of some dead languages. Latin is an example.

46   PROF. GAUNTLETT'S LECTURES.

But modern Latin, *i, e.* Italian, has prepositions. For instance "hominis" and "patribus," in which the prepositions are included in the terminations, are now represented in Italian by the independent prepositions "*del* uomo" and "*degli* padri." To illustrate the fact that a different signification was often implied in the English prepositions in different ages, he read from Abbott's Shakespean Grammar, a few passages dealing with this particular subject.

It is no use trying to master the particles in question by means of grammar. The best thing is repetition and practice. He appreciated Mr. McKenzie's method by which students are taught to hear and speak the same English sentences again and again until they come to get them entirely by heart. They can thus overcome this difficulty to a great extent. The students who first enter his school differ greatly in their knowledge of English. Some can speak tolerably well, while others cannot speak at all. But even in the case of the best students, bad mistakes are often made in the use of prepositions, as : " You are standing behind *of* the table." And he finds his greatest difficulty in this branch of teaching. He usually gives a list of synonymous prepositions and explains their difference by practical examples.

LIST OF PARTIALLY SYNONYMOUS PREPOSITIONS.

In, *into*, inside.
On, over, above, *up*.
Under, beneath, *down*.
Behind.

From.
Before, in front of.
Between.
Across.
Along.
Through.

Across is often misused by students as a verb, as: "He acrossed the river," probably taking it for the verb *cross*. *Across* means going from one side to the other, while *along* means going the length of a place, and *through* going in at one side and out another. To illustrate them by diagrams:

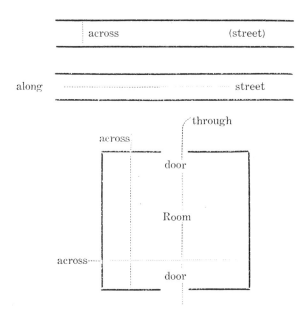

Then he called our attention to the use of *during* and *while*, of which the students have often confused

48   PROF. GAUNTLETT'S LECTURES.

ideas. It is not uncommon for them to speak or write,
as :

"During he stayed in Tokyo......."

To give them clear conception of them, it is better
to give an example or examples in which they are
each properly used, and make them memorize them,
not independently, but together with the words following, as :

"*During the war* I remained in Tokyo."

"*While I was* in Tokyo, the war broke out."

The importance of practice is to be particularly
emphasized in this case. English is a heterogeneous
language ; in other words, it consists of various foreign
elements ; and one has to learn that some verbs take
particular prepositions, by whose use their meaning
is determined. For instance, there is much difference
in the meaning of *hold* in the following three sentences:

He *held* the rope.

He *held on to* the rope. (grasped firmly.)

He *held to* his principles. (remained true to them).

He then explained simply the use of *at*, *on*, and *in*
when relating to time :

At (in any case, some exact point—of time or place.

On (before days).

In (any other period of time).

Japanese students often misuse *from* for *at*, as:

"The meeting will begin from(*at* should be used)six."

From means continuation of time, as "*from* four to
six," and so it cannot be used in such a sentence as
the above.

Other remarks regarding common errors were as
follows :

"To ride *in* (not *on*) a jinrikisha," as we seem to be "enclosed" in it.

"Made *of*" indicates material (not *by* which implies original force or factor.)

"Made *from*" means essence taken from, as: "Wine is made from grapes."

"Aim *at*" (not *for*, which implies *in favor of*.)

Books on grammar recommended were Bain's "English Grammar," and Handbook of English Grammar and Composition for Indian Students "by Macmillan and Hakim. His last suggestion was that we should by all means endeavor to find the original and general import of each preposition.

CHAPTER XI.

CORRECTIONS.

Prof. Gauntlett had it first understood that by " corrections " he did not merely mean those of papers—composition or dictation, but he also meant those of all kinds of mistakes pertaining to all branches of the study of English. He said with truth that correction is a work which is at once laborious and discouraging to the teacher ; it takes a great deal of his time and energy, and yet he gains little or nothing therefrom. The same is particularly the case with lazy students, who only cast a glance over their papers and commit the same blunders again and again, making their teacher feel that the time spent in correcting their papers was wasted. The professor himself had experienced the same feeling until he devised a means by which he could surmound the difficulty to a certain extent ; and he proceeded to give us some idea of his method. He has made a register containing the commonest mistakes made by students in composition, dictation, etc., with numbers affixed to them. These mistakes the students are warned against. He has also made another register with the students' names, and whenever they make any common mistake, he inserts in the blank spaces the numbers corresponding to the mistakes. For instance, if one of the students, named Ito, wrote the capital P below the line, and that mistake had the number 20 fixed to it, he puts the number in thus :

PROF. GAUNTLETT'S LECTURES.

| Ito | 20 | 20 | | | 20 | | | |

By this means, he can warn the students against the repetition of mistakes and make them careful and attentive.

The professor then declared that most of the mistakes which Japanese students make, arise from the difference of manners and customs, manners of thinking, the difference of idioms, and irrregularities of English. To give an example, it is common to find in a letter written by a student, such a sentence as this :

"Do not be anxious about my health." This results from the custom of Japanese letter-writing, in which it is taken for granted that the person addressed would be anxious about the writer's health ; but the idea is different with Englishmen, whose politeness does not go so far. In an advanced class he would give such reasons, but in the case of beginners, he simply tells them not to use such a form. It is also common among Japanese students to begin their letters with the words :

"I have *surely* received your letter." The sentence is correct so far as grammar is concerned, but is not in accordance with the English usage. Englishmen do not use "surely," for the sense conveyed is quite strong enough to their mind without the adverb. "Surely" is invariably used when a little doubt is entertained by a person addressed, as :

A. "Do you think he will come ? "

B. "Yes, I think he will surely come."

Then he came to the common mistake which Japanese students make of the use of "Yes" and "no :"

52   PROF. GAUNTLETT'S LECTURES.

A. "Will you come with us?"
B. "No, I haven't time."
A. "You cannot come?"
B. "No."

They are apt to answer "yes" in such instances, whereas "no" is required once more, because the repetition of the whole answer is understood. It is noteworthy that the Greeks also answer in the same way as the Japanese.

He then called our attention to avoid what he calls "poetical description" of nature with which some Japanese begin their business letters,— letters which must always be brief and to the point. He next referred to one of the systems he uses in teaching composition to beginners. He first tells them a story and then makes them write it, warning them of a few necessary points, such as the tense of the verbs which must be past, etc. If some of them are careless and use verbs in the present tense, he marks the mistakes with "T" (tense) and their eyes open against the repetition of the same blunders.

Make it a rule never to repeat mistakes made by students, for if they hear them twice from your lips, their ears get accustomed to them, and this makes them liable to commit the same blunders again and again. Suppose a student says, "I am very like swimming," instead of "I like swimming very much," it is better to prompt him so as to cause him to find out his mistakes himself. If a student says: "I took my photograph yesterday," Mr Gauntlett says: "Who took your photograph?" Then he will mention a photographer's name, or the name of a friend who took

PROF. GAUNTLETT'S LECTURES. 53

it. He tells him that as he did not take his own
picture, he must say : "I had my photograph taken
yesterday," and he gives him grammatical rules suitable for the occasion. Again if a student replies to a
question, "Can you speak English fluently?" thus :
"No, I can't ; but I hope," he questions him, "What
do you hope?" Then the student will find that he
has made a mistake, and will say, "No, I can't ; but
I wish." Here he gives a simple rule that should
be observed in the use of "hope," and "wish,"
thus :

"If you know the circumstances say 'wish ;' if
don't, use 'hope.'" Then he goes on to correct the
mistake :

"No, I can't ; but I *wish* I could." ("wish," as the
circumstance of "cannot speak fluently" is known.)
"No, I can't ; but I *hope* I shall be able to do so some
day." ("hope," as the future is unknown.)

He also makes the students practise the use of these
two verbs by such examples as : "Has Mr. A come?"
"No, but I hope he will." "Has Mr. B come?" "Yes,
but I wish he had not." And so forth.

Students often use transitive verbs as intransitive,
and *vice versa*. For instance, it is not rare to hear
them say : "The cape pushes into the sea." Tell them
that they can push a table or a desk, but not a cape.
Then they will say "The cape goes out into the sea,"
which is passable. Finally tell them that such a verb
as "project" is the most suitable one in this case. In
like manner, such mistakes as "aim a gun *for*" (at),
etc. should be corrected, telling them that *for* often
contains the idea of help, benefit, and substitution, and

PROF. GAUNTLETT'S LECTURES.

so it cannot be used after " aim a gun," which must always be followed by *at*.

In conversation, it is advisable to train students in the use of direct and indirect narration by asking them questions. You say, pointing to a boy ; " Ask him if he has my book." He will stand up and say to the boy indicated : " If he has my book ? " But such an absurd mistake is made at the beginning only, students gradually learning to ask ; " He has asked me if you have his book," or " Have you his book ? " Inflection and intonation should likewise be practised in conversation. The most important points are :

1. Questions begun with verbs, that is to say, questions answered by " yes " or " no," must be asked with the rising inflection at the end of sentences, as :

    " Are you going to school ? "

2. Indirect questions, which cannot be answered by " yes " or " no," have the falling inflection at the end of sentences like ordinary ones, as :

    " How are you to-day ? "

3. When two direct questions come together, separated by " or," the first has the rising inflection and the last in the falling, as :

    " Which do you like, this or that ? "

    " Will you write that letter, or practise your music ? "

4. Even an indirect question has the rising inflection at the end, when it is repeated, as :

    " What is your name ? "

PROF. GAUNTLETT'S LECTURES.   55

"What is your name?" (when asked twice.)
Then as an illustration of the difference of idiom in
English and Japanese, he gave the following two
sentences :
(To a man ill) "Please take care of yourself."
(Japanese.)
"I hope you will soon be better." (English.)
He next gave a distinct explanation of "ever"
and "once," two adverbs of time, of which Japanese
students have confused ideas.
"Ever" = always, not much used, except in ques-
tions, as :
"Have you *ever* been in Kyoto?"
"He *ever* (always) teaches in this manner."
Once = at a certain time, as :
"I was once in that school."
"Able" and "Suitable."
"Able" can not be used in such a case as the
following : —
"Walls are painted gray ; a color which suits (or
is suitable for) (not *able*) our eyes."
"Also"
"Also" cannot be used in a negative sentence, in
which "either" must be used, as :
"He did not go there *also* (either).
"To-morrow"
"To-morrow" must not be used in the past tense ;
"the next day" or "the following day" should be
used, as :
"He went to Tokyo on the 15th, and *to-morrow*
(the next day, *or* on the following day) to Yokohama."
Pronunciation of numbers.

PROF. GAUNTLETT'S LECTURES.

In pronouncing the Japanese numbers no confusion is caused in sound, but not so with English numbers, especially in the case of the follwing :

$$
\begin{array}{c c}
13 & 30 \\
14 & 40 \\
15 & 50
\end{array}
$$

In pronouncing the numbers in the left-hand column the sound of "n" must be clear and the "ee" long, while in the others, the first syllable must be emphasized, the second being weak.

CHAPTER XII.

CLAUSES AND PHRASES.

" With regard to the subject of clauses and phrases," said the professor, " I have nothing specially new to tell you. To make students familiar with the different forms of clauses and phrases, is a very important factor in pushing them on in composition as well as in conversation. This is particularly the case with subordinate clauses and phrases which perform the function of nouns, adjectives, and adverbs. Perhaps you will find some help in my scheme which I use in exercising my pupils in the analysis of clauses and phrases. I use these marks :

(   )   for noun clauses (or phrases).

$<$ $>$ for adverbial clauses (or phrases).

[   ]   for adjective clauses (or phrases).

⌒‾‾‾‾‾   to underline the verbs governing noun clauses, etc.,

⌃‾‾‾‾   for the words modified by adverbial clauses, etc.,

⌐‾‾‾‾¬   for the nouns modified by adjectives, clauses, etc.,

To give an example :

' We stood $<$ upon the rugged rock $>$ $<$ while the sun was setting $>$.'

Marking thus by brackets prevents confusion. If possible, pencils of different colors should be used in very complex sentences.

58 PROF. GAUNTLETT'S LECTURES.

Care must be taken to warn the students not to mistake co-ordinate clauses for subordinate ones, as :

1. "I took my brother into the waiting-room, when (=and then) in came a policeman and arrested him."

2. <"After proceeding a short distance,> I met

Lord Cawdor, whom (=and him) I recognized at once!"

The professor then wrote on the boards the following examples :

NOUNS.

1. Subject :
(Where he was buried) has never been discovered.

It is evident (that he is mad.)

2. Object of Verb :
I could see (that he was mad.)

3. Object of Preposition :
He was right in (what he said.)

4. Predicate Complement :
He is not (what he appears.)

5. Apposition :
The fact (that he was here) was soon known.

6. Quotations :
("I am tired,") said he.

EXERCISE.

His brother was killed. ⎫
He knew it. ⎪
Three hundred of the ⎬ =
enemy had been taken ⎛
prisoner. ⎪
He did not know it. ⎭

He knew (that his brother
had been killed) but not
(that three hundred of
the enemy had been
taken prisoner.)

Adjectives precede the noun, but adjective clauses come after. In this point Japanese, and I think German also, are more regular, as adjective clauses go before the nouns as : 咋日來た人に會ひました.

ADJECTIVES.

1. Introduced by "who," "which," etc.:
Did you see the tree [that was struck by lightning]?
2. Conjunctive Adverb :
I don't know (when I shall start).

I don't know the time [when I shall start].

EXERCISE.

This is the book.
I gave it to him.

⎫
⎬ =
⎭

This is the book [which I gave (*no* "*it*" *here, a common mistake with Japanese students*) (to) him.]

60   PROF. GAUNTLETT'S LECTURES.

The modifier and the modified should be placed as near as possible. But when there is more than one adverbial clause or phrase, they are often necessarily separated, as :

I have heard (that a law has been made in England,) [by which no ship is allowed to carry gunpowder, dynamite, or any other explosive material without special permission].

ADVERBS.

1. Place :
    Wherever he went > he was welcome.

2. Time :
    While you were speaking > he left the room.

3. Manner :
    I write < as I was taught >.

4. Degree :
    This house is not so large < as we thought it

    was >.
5. Cause :
    Because he was ambitious > I slew him.

6. Consequence :
    He ran so fast < that he could not stop >.

7. Purpose :
    He is running < that he may catch the train >.

PROF. GAUNTLETT'S LECTURES.   61

8. Condition :
      ⟨If he were here⟩, I should ask him.

9. Concession :
      ⟨Though are beaten⟩ we have not lost honor.

The adverb, if it is a good one, can be put in almost any part of a sentence. For instance, in the sentence : "Yesterday I saw Mr. James," "yesterday" can be used thus :

1. Yesterday I saw Mr. James.
2. I yesterday saw Mr. James.
3. I saw yesterday Mr. James.
4. I saw Mr. James yesterday.

But by custom the position of an adverb is generally fixed at the beginning or the end of the sentence. Putting it after a transitive verb should be avoided, for it would, for a moment, seem to be its object. No. 3 in the sentences above mentioned, therefore, is not very good form, neither is No. 2 the best In the case of an adverbial clause or phrase, however, it is to be placed before or after a verb, as :

"To walk in the hot sun, is dangerous ;" or "It is dangerous to walk in the hot sun." Verbs must not be placed at the beginning of a sentence unless in questions or commands, hence the introductory words in "*There* was a man ;" "*It* is to be regretted that he lost his memory." Be sure to have your pupils always understand that every clause or phrase is really a part of speech. A book recommended for students of grammar was :

62   PROF. GAUNTLETT'S LECTURES.

Advanced Lessons in
English Grammar.
By Maxwell.
American Book Company,
New York.

CHAPTER XIV.

FLUENCY IN SPEAKING ENGLISH.

Before commencing his lecture, the professor advised us to examine the papers he referred to on the previous day. He did so in order to let us see some specimens of corrected compositions. I regret to say that the papers in question were given back to the students (5th year class) before I had time to examine them.

The professor then entered upon the assigned topic, saying :

"I have chosen this subject in order to give you some hints for attaining fluency in speaking English. In England we are often asked if we can speak French. "Not fluently," is a common answer. Though French is taught in English schools and many can read and understand that language, those who can speak it with fluency are comparatively few. We can carry on a conversation in French on easy subjects, but if occasion arises to talk on difficult and complicated topics, our fluency ceases, for we have to stop to think of words, phrases, and idioms before we venture to speak. I am convinced that real fluency in speaking a foreign tongue is hardly attainable without hearing foreigners speak and imitating their manner of speaking. Of course we can be understood if we speak slowly and deliberately, and in accordance with grammatical rules. But we must not be content with this; a mere smat-

64   PROF. GAUNTLETT'S LECTURES.

tering of a foreign tongue is within the reach of every-
body.   We must further strive to speak it as naturally
as those to whom the language belongs.   This can only
be done by means of constant repetition of colloquial
forms.   In fact, repetition is the mother of fluency.
I once went to a place where French was spoken, but
as I could not speak French at that time, I had to
depend upon a friend who went with me, as an inter-
preter.   A few years later, I again went to that place.
Meanwhile, I had reviewed my French by means of
grammars and dictionaries, so I thought I could speak
it pretty well.   Having full confidence in my ability to
speak French, I entered a shop and addressed the old
woman there in that language asking the price of
some articles I wanted.   The woman looked at me and
said, with a smile :   "Ah, you are beginning to speak
French now."   I was quite humiliated by this remark
and thought for the first time that dictionaries and
grammars did not make a good speaker, and I realized
the importance of mastering the colloquial language
by practice and repetition."

The professor then spoke of a few important points
which should be observed when aiming at fluency :

1.   To take deep breathing exercises in order to get
    complete control of the voice.

2.   To practise the sentences in *phrases*, not words.

3.   To note what vowels or consonants are obscure,
silent, short, or long.

4.   To make natural combinations of words.

To show by an example :

"He was sitting with his brother on a seat
in front of the school.

PROF. GAUNTLETT'S LECTURES.

Notes : ——— is to show phrases ; vowels or consonants which are either obscure or almost silent ; ⌣ sounds run together.

" There are readers and readers," is a saying commonly quoted in England and America, with regard to the manner of reading, and which suggests much in the way of acquiring fluency. To speak fluently one need not necessarily speak fast. If one observes the points given above and practises repetition steadily, one can soon learn to speak with more or less fluency.

It is a natural characteristic of the English language to insert a consonant, generally " r," at the end of a word ending in a vowel, when the word following also commences with a vowel. For instance, it is a common habit of Englishmen to read such sentences or words as the following as if there were the sound of " r " between :

" I had no idea(r) of going."

" The India(r) Office."

It is of course incorrect to read in such a way, but these instances indicate that it is a natural characteristic of the English language to join the sounds between words.

The next point Japanese students should observe is the use of idioms. There are many idioms which are not now used and care must be taken to choose such as are daily used by Englishmen and Americans. One can tell by the use of idioms whether a speaker is an Englishman or a foreigner, however well he may pronounce his words. Mr. Gauntlett knew a

Japanese gentleman who was a very good speaker of English but who often used idiomatic expressions now slightly out of use, such as "crack jokes," etc. The idiom is not very old, but if an Englishman were to express the same idea, he would simply say "make jokes," which is an everyday expression. Though there are many expressions conveying the idea of "heavy rain," such as, "It is raining heavily (or fast), "there is a great downpour of rain," it is raining in torrents, "etc. the commonest, for force of expression, is, "It's raining cats and dogs!" And the way to master such common idiomatic expressions is to hear Englishmen or Americans speak as often as possible and to learn their manner of speaking through practice and repetition. Here the professor commended Mr. McKenzie's plan of teaching which makes it its aim to repeat the same sentences until the students come to remember them by heart and learn the free use of the phrases in them. He also told of his own experience as a teacher at the Azabu Middle School in which he volunteered to add to his eighteen regular teaching hours of English sixteen extra hours a week. These thirty-four hours were devoted to practical teaching of *beginners* and in five or six months he had the satisfaction of seeing his pupils say and understand many things perfectly which they could not even read. And he recommended that in schools where Englishmen or Americans are employed, their services could be turned to best account by letting them take charge of beginners in pronunciation, accent, etc.

PROF. GAUNTLETT'S LECTURES. 67

If in reading students come across difficult words, such as "astronomical," "latitudinarianism," etc., let them look at them first before they attempt to read, and never let them repeat the *syllables*, for that would bring on a habit of stuttering. Many would read "latitudinarianism" thus : "la—lati—lati—tu—tudinnn—ari—ari—an—arian—ism—ism." Some of the Japanese students read some passages fast and others slowly, like a train running at an irregular speed. They should bear in mind that to be a good reader one is required to read *slowly* first, paying great attention to pauses and inflections of voice, and that practice will enable them to read fluently by and by. The professor read out the following passages from Dickens's "Christmas Carol" in slow, deliberate tones, in order to show us how difficult words should be first carefully divided in syllables.

"Oh! But he was a tight-fisted hand at the grindstone, Scrooge! a squeezing, wrenching, grasping, scraping, clutching, covetous, old sinner! Hard and sharp as flint, from which no steel had ever struck out generous fire."

In French the combination of vowels and consonants between word and word is insisted on more than in English, and the following short sentence shows how this is indicated in elementary French text books.

"Vous_avez_un chien."

He particularly emphasized carrying on the letter "n" at the end of words, saying it should be joined to the next word beginning with a vowel. For the purpose of practising reading he recommended books

PROF. GAUNTLETT'S LECTURES.

in colloquial English, or literary works, such as Macaulay's "History of England," Dickens's "Christmas Carol," and magazines in general.

Vowels are generally sounded too short by Japanese students, whereas in England children have the habit of stretching out, or drawling their sounds. In teaching reading to English children, the teacher warns them time and again, saying "Don't drawl." But the rule might often well be reversed in the case of Japanese students who might better be advised "Drawl." "O" and "a" which are almost diphthongs, must always be pronounced *long,* as in "change" and "no," etc. When we hear a foreigner speak, take note what words have stress and what words are quickly or lightly pronounced. All important words (nouns, verbs, and all modifiers, whether adverb or adjective modifier) have stress. "The" is generally unemphatic, but when it indicates a special thing it is often emphasized, as," That is *the* book," meaning, "That is the best book." Sometimes the accent moves from one syllable to another when a word is used to show some special distinction, as, "He's in*side*, isn't he? "No; he's *out*side."

In teaching grammar, it is advisable to conjugate verbs colloquially and help students to master their use practically, as, "I've; we've; you've; he's (=he has); they've."

Poems may occasionally be memorized with advantage by students: the recitation of them according to their rhythm affords great help in acquiring fluency and a correct accent.

CHAPTER XIV.

CONVERSATION.

Mr. Gauntlett appeared on the platform with three or four books, an ink-bottle, a chalk-box, and a measure under his arm, and said that he was going to give only specimen lessons in conversation, as it was more than he could undertake to go all through any one series of lessons in such a short interval of time. He placed the books on the table, and turning to one of the boy-students, (5th year class) said : "What do you see on the table?" The students addressed, replied, "I see many books." "How many?" asked the professor. "Three," replied the student. "Who knows what this is?" said the lecturer, holding up a measure. Two or three boys replied that they could not give its name in English. But one stood up and said, "A measure." In a similar manner, Mr. Gauntlett went on to ask the English names of an ink-stand, a chalk-box, etc. Then he said : "Where are my books?" "Your books are *on* the table," replied a student. "We don't like," remarked Mr. Gauntlett, "to use the same word twice near together, especially nouns and verbs. Remember that! For instance, in reply to such a question as, "Have you any pens?" to say, "No, I haven't any pens," is not very good English. The last two words should be omitted. He then placed the chalk-box under the desk, and asked : "Where is my chalk-box now?" "It is under the little desk," replied a student.

70   PROF. GAUNTLETT'S LECTURES.

Mr. Gauntlett corrected the student's pronunciation, telling him that " It is under......." should be pronounced like one word, as " It_is_under......," or " i-ti-zunder......" " Where is my chalk-box now?" he asked, placing it behind the books. A student replied, " It is beyond the books," to which reply, he said, " Beyond means far off," making a gesture which made all laugh. Then he placed the chalk-box in front of the books, and asked, " Where is my chalk-box now?" " It is *in front of* the books," came a reply from one of the boys. He called the attention of the audience to the sound of " o " in " front," by saying that " o " preceding " m " or " n " is generally pronounced like " u," as money, ton, son, some, Monday, company, etc. " Where is my chalk-box?" he asked again, putting it between the books and the measure. " It is *between* the books and the measure," replied a student. " Where is my chalk?" he asked, opening the box and showing it. " It is *in* the chalkbox," replied another. Here he explained the use of Material Nouns simply and plainly. " Where did I put it?" he asked, putting chalk into the box, which question was soon answered by someone, who said, " You put it *into* the box." The use of the prepositions " in " (no motion) and " into " (motion) was practically shown by the professor, by pointing to his watch in his pocket, and taking it out and putting it in again. Then he asked the meaning of " to arrange "; but none could answer. Whereupon he told the student that it meant " putting things tidy, or in order." Standing four or five pieces of chalk side by side on the table, he said, " How are they arranged?" " They

PROF. GAUNTLETT'S LECTURES. 71

are arranged in a line," was a reply from one of the students. "Better use "row" (a line of many pieces, as a *row* of desks ; a *row* of soldiers) in this case," he said, and made the student repeat, "They are arranged in a *row*." Then he formed a circle of pieces of chalk, and asked, "How are they arranged?" "They are arranged in a circle," replied a student. And so on.

Prof. "How are they arranged?" (piling up the books.)

Stud. "They are arranged *in a pile*."

Prof. "Where is my hand?" (placing his hand on the books.)

Stud. "It is *on* the books."

Prof. "Where is my hand?" (Keeping it over the books.)

Stud. "It is *over* (or *above*) the books."

Prof. "Where is the measure?" (placing it in front of the books.)

Stud. "It is *in front of* the books." (Note : "In front of" is preferable to "before" which is also used to denote certain relations of *time, superiority, preference*, etc., whereas the former almost always denotes *position*.)

Prof. "Where is my box?" (placing it on the corner of the table.)

Stud. "It is *on the corner* of the table."

Prof. "Where is my box?" (placing it on the centre of the table.)

Stud. "It is on the centre of the table."

Prof. "Where is my box?" (placing it in the corner of the table.)

Stud. "It is *in the corner* of the table."

72   PROF. GAUNTLETT'S LECTURES.

Prof. "Where is my box?" (placing it on the edge of the table.)

Stud. "It is *on the edge* of the table."

Prof. "Where is my stick?" (laying it on the ledge of the blackboard.)

Stud. "It is lying *on the ledge* of the blackboard."

Prof. "Where is my stick?" (leaning it against the table.)

Stud. "It is *leaning against* the table."

Prof. "Where is my box?" (placing it between the books and the ink-bottle.)

Stud. "It is *between* the books and the ink-bottle."

The professor tried to give definite ideas on the use of terms describing positions ; and he did it admirably, prompting and hinting the students by gestures to say exactly what he wanted. It may well be said that this specimen of giving practical lessons in conversation was of more help to us than any other lecture so far delivered.

Mr. Gauntlett told me that he usually gives lessons in something like the following order.

1. Comparison.
2. Measurement.
3. Time by the clock.
4. Newspapers.
5. Prices.
6. Instruments and Machines.
7. Magnetism.
8. Salt.
9. Astronomy.
10. Grammatical Rules (e. g. factitive verbs.)

PROF. GAUNTLETT'S LECTURES.

11. "I wish," "I hope."   "Should," and "Would."
12. Geographical Definitions.
13. Describing the Way.
14. Medical treatment.
    &c.   &c.

CHAPTER XV.

CONVERSATION.

The method by which Prof. Gauntlett gave lessons in conversation this morning was particularly worthy of notice. His distinct pronunciation, ingenious gestures and practical examples with which he prompted the students (5th years course) to speak, were all that could be expected from a teacher of a foreign language. One of the professors remarked in the course of his lectures that "a teacher is born, and not made." If this remark be true, Mr. Gauntlett may well claim to be such. In fact, with one exception I have never seen in Japan so accomplished and well-trained a foreign teacher of English as he.

He first gave several questions similar to the ones he asked last time, and made the students answer, evidently for the purpose of drilling them in the use of prepositions, which formed the subject of his previous lessons.

Prof. "Where are my books?"

Stud. "Two of them are *on* the table and one is *on* the little desk."

Prof. "What is the color of my books?"

Stud. "One is red, and the other two are blue."

Prof. "How big is this book?"

Stud. "It is about eighteen inches long, thirteen inches wide, and three inches thick."

Here he gave the following list of adjectives of

PROF. GAUNTLETT'S LECTURES.   75

measurement and their compound forms, and explained that usually the largest or most important
dimension goes first, and the smallest last :

long .... in length
wide .... in width
thick .... in thickness
high .... in height
deep .... in depth

Prof. " How large is this desk ? "

Stud. " It is about two and a half feet *long* one
foot *wide*, and a foot and a half *high*."

Prof. " How large is this table ? " (pointing at
a student, and measuring it himself.)

Stud. " It is about three feet *in length*, two
(feet) *in width*, and two and a half (feet) *in
height*."

Prof. " What is this ? (showing a measure) And
how long is it ? "

Stud. " It is a measure ; and it is one foot *long*."

Prof. " How many Japanese inches are there in
one foot ? "

Stud. " Ten inches."

Prof. " Now, here is a box, measure it, and tell
me how long it is ? "

Stud. " It's three inches *long*, two (inches) *wide*,
and one (inch) *deep*."

Prof. " Now, ask that student how long that
desk is."

1st Stud. " How long is that desk ? "

2nd Stud. " It's about three feet *in length*, two
in width, and two and a half *in height*."

Prof. " How large is this room ? "

Stud. "It is about a hundred feet *long*, sixty *wide*, and thirty *high*."

Professor Gauntlett then drew a picture of a clock on the board like this:

Prof. "Ask him how big that clock is?"

1st Stud. "How big is that clock?"

2nd Stud. "I think it is two feet *in diameter* and half a foot *in thickness*."

He then wrote the following fractions, and made the students read them in turn:

$\frac{1}{4}$ (one-fourth or a quarter) $\frac{1}{3}$ (one-third or a third.)

$\frac{1}{2}$ (one-half or a half) $\frac{1}{5}$ (one-fifth or a fifth.)

$\frac{1}{16}$ (one-sixteenth or a sixteenth) $\frac{2}{7}$ (two-sevenths.)

$2\frac{1}{7}$ (two and one-seventh.)

He next taught them to tell the time by the clock by changing the positions of the hands of the clock he had drawn, as:

PROF. GAUNTLETT'S LECTURES.

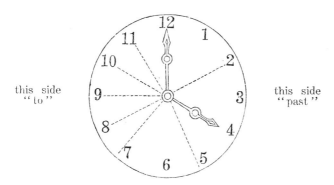

this side "to"

this side "past"

Prof. "What time is it now by this clock?"
Stud. "It is twelve o'clock."
Prof. "What time is it now?"
Stud. "Half past three."
Prof. "What time is it now?"
Stud. "(A) quarter past one."
Prof. "What time is it now?"
Stud. "Ten (minutes) to three."

Several expressions are used in asking the time:
1. "What o'clock is it now?" (old.)
2. "What is the time?" (common.)
3. "What time is it?" (common.)

Prof. "What time is it now?" (drawing the longer hand very near twelve.)

Stud. "It is almost (or nearly) three."

Writing "4.20 p. m." on the board the professor said, "Suppose you were going to leave Kanazawa by train for Tokyo. We can say, 'I shall go by the *fast, through, express*) train.' We may use 4.20 P.M. as an adjective as well, and say, 'I shall go by the *four twenty P.M.* train.'"

CHAPTER XVI.

CONVERSATION.

The professor drew the map of part of Scotland to begin with:

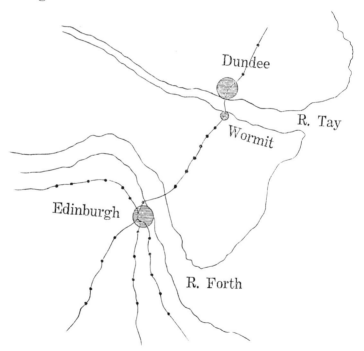

After briefly explaining the map, that the red lines indicated the railways and the small dots, small stations, he told the following story of a railway accident, in clear, distinct English:

PROF. GAUNTLETT'S LECTURES. 79

"About thirty or forty years ago, an express was running from Edinburgh to the north. It was the night-express, which generally ran from that city to Dundee without stopping at the smaller stations. The distance between the two cities is some forty miles. It was the night of the 24th of December. The following day being a great holiday in England, there were in the train several hundred passengers returning home. Unfortunately the weather was stormy. The snow was several feet deep and the wind was blowing a gale. Over the River Tay there was a wooden bridge, two miles long, and not very strongly built. Well, the train stopped at Wormit. The station-master said to the engine-driver: "Why have you stopped here?" "The weather is bad," he replied, "and so I am afraid to go over the bridge." Thereupon the station-master telegraphed to Dundee to ask if the bridge was safe. 'It seems to be all right, for the telegraph lines are safe,' was the reply. The engine-driver, still feeling uneasy, said to the stoker: "You get down from the engine, and go over the bridge before the train, and examine it. The stoker did so, and the train slowly followed him. He was almost at the other side of the river, when he heard a great crash. Much astonished at the noise, he went back. He soon found that the centre of the bridge had given way and the train had fallen into the river. By this accident about six hundred lives were lost. It was one of the worst accidents ever recorded." While he was speaking, the professor, with his stick continually referred to the map he had drawn, seemingly to arouse a vivid imagination in

PROF. GAUNTLETT'S LECTURES.

his pupils' minds. He also stopped at every difficult word he used, and gave a full explanation of it. When he had finished telling the story, he asked the boys questions concerning it, one by one, thus :

Prof. "When did this accident occur ?"

Stud. "It occurred on the night of the 24th of December, about thirty years ago."

Prof. "Where did it take place?"

Stud. "Near Wormit, in Scotland."

Prof. "Did the accident happen to an express or to an ordinary train?"

Stud. "It happened to an express."

Prof. "What express was it?"

Stud. "It was the night-express."

Prof. "In what direction was it running?"

Stud. "From Edinburgh to the north."

Prof. "What is an express?"

Stud. "It is a train which runs fast, and does not generally stop at any small stations."

Prof. "And an ordinary train?"

Stud. "An ordinary train is one which generally stops at every station."

Prof. "How was the weather?"

Stud. "It was stormy."

Prof. "Who stopped the train at Wormit Station?"

Stud. "The engine-driver."

Prof. "Why did he do so?"

Stud. "To see if the bridge was safe, because he was afraid to cross it."

Prof. "Why were there so many people in the train?"

PROF. GAUNTLETT'S LECTURES.

Stud. Because the next day was a great holiday."
And so he went on until the bell rang. On the 10th,
Prof. Gauntlett was to give lessons to the boys in
Composition, and he told them to write the story
of the railway accident which formed the topic of
conversation that day. In writing a composition, the
following remarks were made by him:

1. Write "*Composition*" on the first line (or at
the top of the paper), and "The Fifth year
Class (or Class V). Aug. 10th, 1904." below, and
the name on the same line, as:

COMPOSITION.

Class V.   *Aug. 10th, 1904.*   *Name.*

2. Write on alternate lines.
3. All use paper of the same size.
4. Write very carefully and neatly.

After the class the two professors, Messrs. Gauntlett
and McKenzie taught us the national anthem of
England.

Then Mr. Gauntlett sang a traditional song of Wales,
the tune of which seemed old and wierd. The words
were as follows:

THE DEATH OF ST. DAVID.

I.

David the Bard on his bed of death lies,
Pale are his features and dim are his eyes.
Yet all around him his glance wildly roves—
Till it alights on the harp that he loves.

II.

Give me my harp, my companion so long,
Let it once more add its voice to my song.
Tho' my old fingers are palsied and weak,
Still my good harp for its master will speak.

III.

Often the hearts of our chiefs it has stirred,
When its loud summons to battle was heard ;
Harp of my country, dear harp of the brave,
Let thy last notes hover over my grave ?

Mr. Gauntlett sang the same song in Welsh, which was Greek to us.

CHAPTER XVII.

COMPOSITION.

The professor made three of the boys (5th year course) write on the boards their compositions about the railway accident, the story of which he told them at the previous conversation lesson. The following are the compositions they wrote, with the professor's marks for correction, which he caused the boys to make afterwards by hints and suggestions:

I.

About thirty or foŭrty years ago, the following accident happened in Scotland. On the 24th. of December, a night express was runing from Edinburgh to the north. This train had many passengers, Because the next night was a great Holiday, and they were going to their homes.

II.

About thirty-five or foŭrty years ago, it happened in Scotland,- a terrible sorrowful accident, in which killed a great many people. Now the night were

84 PROF. GAUNTLETT'S LECTURES.

Express which started ~~∧~~ from Edinburgh was running

D
northly to Qundee ~~(in-the-dark)~~. The falling snow,

flake by flake, accumulated on the ground about two

feet, and ~~the~~ there was a great storm whose fierce

blast pierced the train through, like a dart.

III

I shall tell you of a terrible railroad accident that

e
happend in Scotland about thirty or fourty years

lies to the north
ago. Scotland ~~is-a-northern-state~~ of England. The

situated
capital is called Edinburgh, which is ~~along~~ by the

R   a
southern bank of the river Forth, And it is connected

by the railway with Dundee, which is a large city

R
on the northern bank of the ~~famous~~ river Tay. On

village
the opposite bank there is a ~~city~~ named Wormit

where there is a station.

After pointing out mistakes in writing, spelling, custom, and grammar in the compositions of four or five boys, the professor told all the boys to write their compositions again by the next composition hour.

CHAPTER XVIII.

CONVERSATION.

The professor drew on the board the pictures of a hill, a temple, and an arch and then told the boys (5th year course) the following story in common idiomatic English, clearly explaining every word which he thought they could not understand:

"Once upon a time, there were two Chinamen called Chang and Chong. One evening they went to a party at a friend's house. While they were there, Chang began to boast (to speak in a proud manner) about his eyesight. (ability to see, power of seeing, as: far-sighted, near-sighted, long-sighted, short-sighted) 'I have excellent eyesight,' he said, 'I can distinctly see small things at a great distance.' 'My eyesight is much better than yours,' broke in Chong, 'I can see things which you cannot.' Hearing this, Chang got very angry, and insisted that he could see better than Chong who also declared that he could see better than the former, till at last the two began to quarrel. 'It's bad to quarrel at a friend's,' said one of their companions. 'To-morrow you two had better test (examine, prove) your eyesight. There is a temple on a hill outside the city. In front of the temple is a monument. Now the one of you who can read the inscription (words) on the monument from the greater distance, shall be said to have the better eyesight.' The two Chinamen agreed to do so, and went home.

86   PROF. GAUNTLETT'S LECTURES.

That evening, at nine o'clock, Chang took a lantern,
a box of matches, a pencil, and paper, and slowly
left his house and went right up to the temple.
He lighted the lantern and copied the inscription
on the monument, which ran thus : ' This monument
was erected in memory of the great soldier, Go
Bang.' He then went back home and read the
writing over a hundred times until he had it by
heart. He was very dishonest. But Chong, about
midnight, did exactly the same thing. Chong got
closer to the monument and wrote down not only
the principal inscription, but a line in smaller letters
under it, ' Erected in the year 1001.' He also read
the writing again and again, until he also remembered
it perfectly. Well, the next day, at about twelve,
that friend called on Chang and Chong, and took them
to the hill on which the temple stood. When they
got to the arch, Chang suddenly stopped and said,
' I can see the inscription on the monument from
here,' and he read in a loud voice, ' This monument
was erected in memory of the great soldier, Go Bang. '
' What wonderful eyesight you have ! ' cried the
friend in astonishment ; for he could not even see
the monument. But Chong proudly said, ' Is that all
you can read, Chang ? I can see some smaller words
written below what you have just read : " Erected
in the year 1001." ' Chang declared that there were
no such words, while Chong insisted there were, so
that at last they again began to quarrel. The friend
did not know what to do, but fortunately the priest
of the temple just then happened to come towards
them. ' Look here ! This priest is a good man, and

PROF. GAUNTLETT'S LECTURES. 87

will not tell a lie,' said the friend, 'so you had better
ask him which of you is right.' So they followed
his advice. When the priest had heard what they
said, he said, 'Gentlemen, you have very, very wonderful eyesight. The monument was taken away this
morning, and is now behind the temple!'"

The professor then proceeded to ask the boys
questions about the story and make them answer as
he did on the previous occasion, as:

Prof.　"Where were Chang and Chong?"

Stud.　"They were at a friend's house."

Prof.　"Why were they at a friend's?"

Stud.　"They were at a party."

Prof.　"While they were there, what did Chang
begin to do?"

Stud.　"He began to boast of his eyesight."

Prof.　"What did Chong say to Chang?"

Stud.　"He said: 'My eyesight is much better
than yours.'"

Prof.　"Then what did they begin to do?"

Stud.　"They began to quarrel."

Prof.　"What did one of the friends say to them?"

Stud.　"He said, 'Don't quarrel.'"

Prof.　"What did he advise them to do?"

Stud.　"He advised them to stop quarreling, and
test their eyesight."

Prof.　"How were they to test their eyesight?"

Stud.　"By reading the inscription on a monument from the greatest possible distance."

Prof.　"Well, what did Chang do that night?"

Stud.　"He went to the temple and copied the
inscription."

PROF. GAUNTLETT'S LECTURES.

Prof. "When he had copied it, what did he do?"

Stud. He went back home, and read it a hundred times, until he remembered it by heart.

Prof. "Was Chang honest?"

Stud. "No, he was dishonest."

Prof. "Who came to their houses to take them to the temple?"

Stud. "The same friend that had advised them to stop quarreling."

And so questions and answers went on.

After the classes, Mr. Gauntlett told us a story, according to a promise he had made the preceding day. By the telling of this story, which was a fairy tale, he evinced another talent—that of story-telling. While he went on with his story, with gesticulations, and imitation of the voice of different characters, the whole room was in profound silence, the audience being spell-bound, so to speak, by his inimitable elocution. Should he appear with a fan in his hand on the platform of a *yose*—if I may be allowed to make such a remark—and tell stories in Japanese, the leading story-tellers of Japan, would have a strong rival in him. The gist of the story is as follows:

A great many years ago, there lived in a lonely part of England, an old man, who was more than hundred years old, and his only grandson, a boy of about twelve. Their house, which stood far from any village, was a large square building with high, small windows. They always lived in one room, near the entrance, and all the other rooms were unknown to

PROF. GAUNTLETT'S LECTURES.

Jack, for such was the boy's name ; and the old man always kept the door leading to them locked.

"Jack," said the old man one day to his grandson, "I am going to London, and I have to stay there some days, during which time you must study diligently, and never try to get into the other rooms." "But what about my meals, grandpa?" asked the boy. "Don't trouble yourself about your meals ; somebody will bring them to you." So the old man started on his journey, leaving the boy alone in the house.

Jack studied some hours until he began to feel hungry ; it was dinner time. He went to the window, thinking that somebody from the next village would bring his dinner. He waited and waited, but no one came. Impatience and hunger drove the boy from the window back to the table, and he was about to sit down, when his eye rested upon a glass of water and a plate of stale bread on the table. He drank the water and devoured the bread, and kept glancing on all sides wondering who would take the glass and plate away. The things, however, disppeared while he was thus looking around, when or how he could not tell. So the meals appeared and disappeared.

This went on for several days, meals as bad as ever. Jack's curiosity was now at the highest pitch ; he thought there was something in the unknown rooms that caused the mystery. In spite of his grandfather's words, he determined to open the forbidden door. Finding a key to the door in the pocket of his grandfather's ulster, which was hanging on a peg, he put it into the keyhole, turned it, opened the door, and entered the room. It was a large, dark room with a floor made of flag-stones. But what made Jack timid, were the skins and bones of animals and fishes which were heaped up on the shelves around the room. Bats were flying about in the semi-darkness and owls, serenely perched on the skeletons, looked at Jack with their big, sleepy eyes. But the most wonderful part of the story has yet to be told. In the middle of the room there was a table, on which was a big, heavy book.

Jack, recovering his composure, approached the table and opened the book. It was in Latin. Now Jack having a little knowledge of Latin, began to read,— "abracadabra." He had scarcely finished this mysterious word, when somebody struck him on the right shoulder. He turned round in astonishment, but there was nobody to be seen! He supposed he had been struck by a bat, and so read the word again, when he was struck on the left shoulder! He turned round again, but nobody was there! Plucking up his courage, Jack again read. This time he received a severe blow on both shoulders! He again turned his head, and saw an old, old man with long beard. He had a tall, pointed hat on, and brooms in place of legs. "You have read that word, haven't you?" questioned the old man. "Yes, but I will never read it again," replied Jack, crying. "You have read it three times?" Yes, but I will never read it again." "You have; then I will be your slave and do exactly what you order me." Thereupon Jack stopped crying and soon putting on proud airs, said, "Bring me some good soup first, then." And the soup appeared on the table like a flash of lightning. "Beefsteak,

PROF. GAUNTLETT'S LECTURES.

vegetables and sauce." And they appeared in a twinkling. "Apple pie," cried Jack again, "and mind you bring it hot!" And it was produced before his eyes. He put a spoonful into his mouth, but it was so hot that it burnt his mouth. "Oh, oh, oh! Make haste and bring me a mouthful of water," cried Jack in agony. The strange old man soon produced a tiny tumbler containing just a mouthful. Jack tossed it off, and cried in an angry tone, "You rascal! Bring me more water! Bring all the water you can find." Immediately twenty old men appeared, each with a big bucket full of water in his hand. Jack was astonished and said; Stop! Stop! "Not so much!" "This is only small quantity; you ordered me to bring all the water I could find, and I shall do exactly what you tell me. All the water of the rivers, lakes, seas, and oceans must be brought." "Oh, help! help!" cried the poor boy in despair. But bucket after bucket was poured on the floor until it was so deep that he was obliged to stand on the chair. The water rose higher and higher and Jack got on the table. Still the water rose! Then he placed the chair on the table and stood on it. But the water rose to his waist, then up to his chest, then to throat, then to his mouth, and then to his nose. He was on the point of being suffocated, when his own cries awoke him from his sleep, for it was only a dream!

CHAPTER XIX.

CONVERSATION.

The topic of conversation was "prices," and his method of teaching was, as usual, interesting. Questions and answers between the professor and the students (5th year course) were as follows :

Prof. "What does milk cost in Kanazawa?"

Stud. "It costs two *sen* a *go*."

Prof. "Why did I underline "*sen*" and "*go*?"

Stud. "Because they are not English. Foreign words are generally underlined."

Prof. "Can you explain the difference in meaning between ' it costs,' and ' it cost'?"

Stud. "The former is the present tense and the latter the past."

Prof. "What is the difference in meaning between 'It costs 2 *sen* for one *go*', and ' It costs 2 *sen* a *go*?"

Stud. (Could not answer.)

Prof. "Well, in the first sentence it is implied that the price might be different when we buy more than one *go*. In the second, no such sense is implied ; whatever quantity we may buy the price is fixed, that is to say, we get a thing at the same rate."

Prof. "Is there any coal in Japan?"

Stud. "Yes, it is found in many places.

Prof. "What does it cost?"

Stud. "I think it costs ten *yen* a ton."

PROF. GAUNTLETT'S LECTURES.   93

Prof.   " What does Japanese wine cost ? "

Stud.   " It costs ten *sen* a *go.* "

Prof.   " What does ink cost ? "

Stud.   " It costs five *sen* a bottle.

Prof.   " Liquids, as wine and milk are mostly sold in England by the ' pint,' which is about $2\frac{2}{3}$ *go*."

Prof.   " What do pencils cost ? "

Stud.   " They cost twenty *sen* a dozen."

Prof.   " Pencils, pens, and a hundred other articles are sold by the ' gross ' in England and America.   A gross is twelve dozen (144).

Prof.   " What do pens cost ? "

Stud.   " I think they cost one (*yen* and) forty (*sen*) a gross."

Prof.   " What does silk cost in Japan ? "

Stud.   " It cost one *yen* a yard.

Prof.   " Silk and other stuffs are sold by the yard or the foot."

Prof.   " Do you know what compasses are ? What are they used for ? "

Stud.   " They are used for drawing."

Prof.   " What do they cost ? "

Stud.   " They cost two *yen* a set (or a box)."

Prof.   " What does chalk cost ? "

Stud.   " It costs twenty *sen* a box. (Here the professor told an interesting account of his native town which is rich in coal and of the town to which he was sent to school, which abounds in chalk. He also told us that England was called " Albion " by the ancient Romans, because its coast looked white.)

Prof.   " What, in your opinion, is the best newspaper in Japan ? "

49   PROF. GAUNTLETT'S LECTURES.

Stud.   " I think the *Jiji* and the *Nippon* are the best."

Prof.   " What does the *Jiji* cost ? "

Stud.   " It costs forty *sen* a month."

Prof.   " What does the best Japanese tea cost ? "

Stud.   " It costs one *yen* a pound.

Prof.   " There are two principal meanings of the word ' pound.' Mention them."

Stud.   " One means a weight and the other a coin.

Prof.   You often see in English or American papers or magazines the letters, ' £ ' and ' lb.' They both stand for ' pound,' and are abbreviations of the Latin word ' libra ' which was the name of an old Roman weight. ' £ ' is used for money, as : £ 1,000 (one thousand pounds); ' lb ' indicates a pound weight, as : 10 lbs. of tea.

' $ ' for ' dollar ' is a combination of the initials of the United States : U. S.

' £ ' ' $ ' ' ¥ ' (Yen) always precede figures, as : £ 5,000 : $ 700,000 :   ¥ 500.

QUESTIONS.

Ques.   What are the best text-books of English for the middle schools, especially for the 4th or 5th classes ?

Ans.   This is a very difficult question to answer ! I would recommend

1.   Selections from standard authors,
2.   Books in colloquial style,
3.   Interesting books,

PROF. GAUNTLETT'S LECTURES.

In consideration of these points the following is to be recommended :

SELECT STORIETTES (SANSEIDO).

Ques. What do you think of "Pushing to the Front"?

Ans. The style is good, but it is fitted more to be used as a text-book of ethics, than English.

Ques. What are the best " vertical " copy-books?

Ans. I should say Jackson's. They can be had at Kelly and Walsh's, Yokohama.

CHAPTER XX.

CONVERSATION.

The professor collected the compositions written by the 5th year students, and said that the corrections would be made by the third hour the next day, and that the teacher-students might examine the papers to see how they were corrected, before they were returned to the boys. Then he informed the students that he would give lessons in conversation in place of composition changing the order of the programme.

"I will tell you a story," he said, "which is quite different from the last one. The story I am going to tell you is a true one." So saying, he wrote the following words on the board and explained their meanings :

Gelert (the name of a hound.)

Llewelyn (King of Wales, who lived about nine hundred years ago.)

King John (King of England, who lived at the same time.)

hound (a dog used for hunting.)

wedding (marriage.)

game (animals or birds killed by huntsmen.)

trail (a mark on the ground, such as those made by animals walking.)

blood (the red liquid which flows through our bodies).

stained (marked or colored.)

hilt (*explained by a picture.*)

PROF. GAUNTLETT'S LECTURES.

remorse (a feeling of sorrow for guilt.)
monument (explained in a former lesson.)
Beddgelert (the name of a village.)
Snowdon (the name of a mountain.)

Having thus made the preparatory explanations, he proceeded to tell the story :

"Once upon a time, there lived in England a King named John, who was not a very good King. He was King for only a few years. At the same time, there was a king in Wales called Llewelyn. Llewelyn was a pretty good King, and strong in battle. The two Kings were friends. Llewelyn married the daughter of King John, who gave him as a wedding present a beautiful dog, which was quick and faithful. The name of that dog was Gelert. King Llewelyn was very fond of hunting, and he had many hounds, but none were so strong or quick as Gelert. Whenever he went to the mountains to hunt, he took Gelert with him. One day when he was starting from his castle to hunt, Gelert was not to be found. The King called him again and again, but he did not come. Then his soldiers went into the castle to look for him but could find him nowhere. So the King went out hunting without Gelert, but unfortunately got very little game. Well, the King was very much disappointed, and towards evening returned to his castle. When he got near the gate, Gelert came out to meet him, wagging his tail ; but his body and neck were covered with blood, and a trail of blood went into the castle. The King could not understand it ; so he followed the trail and it led him into the bed-room of his little child. The room was in confusion. The

PROF. GAUNTLETT'S LECTURES.

bed, floor, and bed-clothes were stained with blood, but the child was nowhere to be seen. At this sight, King Llewelyn got very angry. Taking his sword he stuck it into Gelert's heart, up to the hilt, and killed him ; but at that moment he heard the voice of his child. He lifted up the bed-clothes, and there was his child, quite safe and smiling. The King looked round and found behind the bed a huge wolf, dead. Then he understood the whole matter. Gelert had seen the wolf coming to the child and had attacked it to save his young master, and killed it. The King was full of remorse. He took the dead body of Gelert and buried it on the top of a mountain near his castle. Over the grave he built a large and beautiful monument of marble.

This event took place about nine hundred years ago ; yet if you go to the village called Beddgelert' you will still find the hill, and on it the monument, though now very little remains of it."

Questions and answers between the professor and the students then followed :

Prof. "When did this event take place?"

Stud. "It took place about nine hundred years ago."

Prof. "And where?"

Stud. "In Wales."

Prof. "Where is Wales?"

Stud. "It is in Great Britain."

Prof. "Who was the King of Wales at that time?"

Stud. "King Llewelyn."

Prof. "What sort of King was he?"

PROF. GAUNTLETT'S LECTURES. 99

Stud. "He was a pretty good king."

Prof. "And who was King of England?"

Stud. "King John."

Prof. "What kind of man was he?"

Stud. "He was not very good."

Prof. "Whom did King Llewelyn marry?"

Stud. "He married the daugter of King John."

Prof. "Did King John give him any wedding present?"

Stud. "Yes, he made him a present of a fine hound, called Gelert."

Prof. "What was King Llewelyn's favorite amusement?"

Stud. "It was hunting."

Prof. "What kind of dog was Gelert?"

Stud. "It was a quick, faithful dog."

Prof. "Well, one day when King Llewelyn was starting out hunting, what happened?"

Stud. "Gelert could not be found."

Prof. "Who searched for him?"

Stud. "His soldiers."

Prof. "King Llewelyn went up the mountain to hunt without Gelert. What was the result? Was he successful?"

Stud. "No, he caught hardly any game."

Prof. "When he returned to his castle in the evening, did he see Gelert?"

Stud. "Yes, the hound came out to meet him."

Prof. "What did the King notice?"

Stud. "He noticed that Gelert was covered with blood."

Prof. "What else did he notice?"

PROF. GAUNTLETT'S LECTURES.

Stud. "He noticed a trail of blood."

Prof. "Where did the trail go?"

Stud. "It went into the castle."

Prof. "When the King saw the trail, what did he do?"

Stud. "He followed it."

Prof. "Where did it lead him?"

Stud. "It led him into his child's bed-room."

Prof. "In what condition was the bed?"

Stud. "It was in confusion and covered with blood."

~~~~~~~~~~~~~~~~~~~~

QUESTIONS.

Ques. "Who was the originator of vertical writing?"

Ans. "I cannot answer this question. The style was used in the Elisabethan age. In fact it was the only style in some past times."

Ques. "What is the difference in pronunciation of 'er' 'ir,' and 'ur'?"

Ans. Practically no difference in England. In America 'er' and 'ir' are pronounced a little weaker than 'ur,' but there is very little distinction."

After the lessons were over, Prof. Gauntlett told us a story for our amusement. He wrote on the board:

Mr. Jones   Mary (the daughter)

Mrs. Jones   Robinson (servant)

Tom (the son)   Granny (an old woman)

"Imagine yourselves present at a social party in

PROF. GAUNTLETT'S LECTURES. 101

England or in America," he said, " for the story I am
going to tell you is a specimen of those told on such
occasions." He then began his story :

Many years ago, there lived in Texas, America, a
well known lawyer by the name of Jones. He was a
fine, respectable gentleman, but had one peculiarity,
that is, *his lower lip stuck out and so he had a singular way of speaking* (imitated). His wife was a tall,
fine woman, much respected by the neighbors, for she
was kind to the poor, but she had also one peculiarity,
that is, *her upper lip stuck out, which made her speak
in this fashion* (imitated). Their son, Tom, who liked
sports rather than study, had also one peculiarity ; that
is, *his mouth was always open on the right side*
(imitated). Their daughter Mary, a pretty girl of
twelve, had likewise one peculiarity ; that is, *her mouth
was always open on the left side* (imitated). Their servant, Robinson, stuttered, so they were a strange
household as regard their way of speaking. There was
an old, superannuated servant in their house, called
" Granny," and though supposed to be of no use, she
was the only one who could talk straight."

The story which followed is better seen than described, as the amusement consisted in Mr. Gauntlett's
imitation of their styles to talking. Finally, when
about to retire for the night, not one of the family was
able to blow out the candle—not even Robinson ! They
finally called " Granny," who did not waste her breath
in any useless attempts to extinguish it but did it with
a fan.

CHAPTER XXI.

CONVERSATION.

The professor criticised the compositions written by the 5th year boys. The chief suggestions are mentioned below :

1. " The station master asked, ' Why have you stopped the train ? ' " Such a sentence as that above referred to is better changed to the indirect narration, as in A, or the order might be altered as in B.

A. " The station master asked him why he had stopped the train."

B. " ' Why have you stopped the train ? ' asked the station-master."

2. If possible, use no exclamative sentence, which though often used in conversation, is seldom used in composition. " What was his astonishment on seeing it ! " The preceding sentence should, therefore, be changed to an ordinary declarative sentence, as :

" He was extremely astonished on seeing it."

3. Care must be taken, not only in punctuating, but in writing the punctuation marks, properly, as :

" Class V ; " not " Class V ¸ "

4. The Past Perfect Tense is always *more past* than the Past Tense, and denotes the completion of an action *before* the time of another past action, as :

" I *had written three letters* before my brother *arrived.*"

PROF. GAUNTLETT'S LECTURES. 103

There is no need whatever to use the Past Perfect Tense in a sentence such as this : "About forty years ago a bad accident *had* happened."

The professor then related the following story :

COOLHEAD AND BOASTER.

Coolhead and Boaster were two friends. The one was about fifty years of age and the other twenty. Coolhead was quite a brave man, but Boaster very proud. One day these two men were walking through a forest. It was winter time and the snow lay two or three inches deep on the ground. " Do you see those footprints ? " asked Coolhead, suddenly stopping. " What animal do you think made them ? " " I expect they were made by a bear or a wolf," answered Boaster. " Then let us go home," said Coolhead, " we have no weapons and are in danger of losing our lives." " No fear of that," said Boaster proudly, " I will help you. I will kill any animal that comes." As they went on, they saw more footprints. " There must be many animals ! " cried Coolhead again. " You need not be anxious," said Boaster, again, " I will kill even a bear." Just at that moment, they heard the roar of a wild animal, and a huge bear came out from behind the trees. Do you think Boaster helped Coolhead? No ; he climbed up a tree and left his poor friend to meet the danger alone. Coolhead who was old and weak could neither run away nor climb a tree ; so he threw himself down flat on the snow, because he knew that no animal would eat a dead man. So he pretended to be dead. Well, the bear came up to him and sniffed all around him, sometimes putting his nose so near Coolhead's ear that

104 PROF. GAUNTLETT'S LECTURES.

he could feel its warm breath. The bear thought that he was dead and went away. Boaster then came down from the tree, feeling very much ashamed of his cowardly action. "What did the bear whisper to you," asked he, thinking to pass over the matter as a joke. "He said, 'Boaster is a bad man,'" replied Coolhead.

Questions and answers followed as usual :

Prof. "Have you ever heard this story before?"

Stud. "No, it is the first time I've ever heard it."

Prof. "Were those men relations?"

Stud. "No, they were friends."

Prof. "What time of the year was it?"

Stud. "It was winter time."

Prof. (to another student,) "He said it was winter time. Was he right?"

Stud. "Yes, he was right."

Prof. "How do you know it was winter?"

Stud. "Because snow lay on the ground."

Prof. "Was the snow very deep?"

Stud. "No, it was only two inches deep."

Prof. "What kind of man was Coolhead?"

Stud. "He was a brave man."

Prof. "Was Boaster a brave man, too?"

Stud. "No, he was a proud, but cowardly man."

Prof. "Were they of the same age?"

Stud. "No, Coolhead was about fifty years old and Boaster twenty."

Prof. "As they were going along, what did Coolhead see?"

Stud. "He saw some footprints in the snow.

Prof. "What footprints were they?"

Stud. "They were the footprints of some animal."

PROF. GAUNTLETT'S LECTURES. 105

Prof. "When Coolhead saw them, what did he say to Boaster?"

Stud. "He said he wanted to go home."

Prof. "Then how did Boaster reply?"

Stud. "He replied that he would kill the animal and help Coolhead."

Prof. "After a short time, what did they hear?"

Stud. "They heard the roar of a wild animal."

Prof. "A few minutes after, what did they see?"

Stud. "They saw a large bear."

Prof. "Where was the bear coming from?"

Stud. "It was coming out from behind a tree."

Prof. "Then did Boaster keep his promise?"

Stud. "No, he climbed up a tree without helping Coolhead."

Prof. "What did Coolhead do?"

Stud. "He threw himself flat on the snow.

Prof. "Why did he not climb a tree?"

Stud. "Because he was too old to do so."

Prof. "Why did he throw himself on the ground?'

Stud. "Because he knew that no animal would eat a dead man."

Prof. "What did the bear do?"

Stud. "It went up to Coolhead and put its nose close to his ear."

Prof. "How did Coolhead answer Boaster's question?"

Stud. "He answered that the bear had whispered to him: 'Boaster is a bad man'."

PROFESSOR McKENZIE'S LECTURES.

CHAPTER I.

THE GOUIN SYSTEM.

Mr. McKenzie came ten minutes behind time, the reason for which he ascribed to several derailments of the tram-car he took from Kanaiwa, where he and the other two professors are stopping. His subject this morning was to be *The Gouin System,* but in reality he spoke very little about it, speaking rather of the historical development of language education. He said he believed it was Garfield who wisely said that if he had only a log cabin and a bench, with Mark Hopkins at one end of the bench, and himself at the other, that would be all the university he would ask for. The question of education depends very much upon the teacher who guides, and the student who learns. If the former is capable and sympathetic, and the latter eager and faithful, the result will be satisfactory. In Socrates' time, there were in Greece neither printing-presses nor printed books, but there appeared in succession a great number of scholars of the highest intellectual attainments. It is thus seen that if teacher and pupil are of the right kind the work of education may be accomplished with any book or no book. Some men can carve a boat or the figure of a man with a penknife as well as others who have all the usual tools. But what is possible may not always be advisable. The question of choosing the *best* way to attain any object is very important. Now, there are many ways in which we may go from Kanazawa to Toyama ; for example, on horseback, or by stage, *jinrikisha*, or train. But most people prefer the train, because by means of it they can travel much faster and more comportably than by the other means. We can travel many times as fast as our ancestors did a hundred years ago. It is the same with education. What they learned in twenty years in former days, can be compressed into five years or so now-a-days. About forty years ago when he was a boy, children when they entered school were set at once to study the alphabet and then the readers, etc. But now the kindergarten, initiated by Froebel, introduces them to knowledge in various ways which interest them. Again, when he was a schoolboy, teachers ruled their pupils in an autocratic manner, and those who disobeyed or neglected their lessons were whipped. The system of education that prevailed in the early part of last century in America and England was one of force, so to speak, and children were driven to the acqiurement of knowledge by scolding and whipping. But now a teacher is a friend to lead the children. When he started to learn Latin, after a short time at the grammar, he was made to begin at such difficult works as those of Caesar and Cicero. With Greek it was the same, being put directly at such authors as Xenophon and Homer, as soon as he had gone through a short course of grammar. This is the way the last generation was obliged to go in learning the dead languages. Nor was there a much better method by which to learn the living ones. But now-a-days things are changed. Some years ago Dr. Harper of Chicago University published a series of books

108   PROF. McKENZIE'S LECTURES.

introducing improved methods for studying the dead
languages, by using which the student can acquaint
himself with these languages in a shorter space
of time and with greater ease and certainty than
by the old methods. Macaulay said, in effect, of these
old systems : " Not one of them teaches a real living
language."

By the classical method it is doubtful if one can ever
learn to speak fluently in a foreign language. But if
thoroughly taught according to the best modern methods, one can get to speak readily in a foreign tongue in
a few years. By good modern methods he meant such
systems as teach foreign languages in a manner somewhat similar to that by which children naturally learn
to speak their mother tongue. How does a carpenter
teach his apprentice and make a carpenter of him?
By giving him lectures on the use of tools? By means
of a book describing their uses? He does *not* do that ;
he makes him go directly to the use of the tools. The
apprentice may make mistakes, but he will learn. The
student learning a language by the orthodox method
has been studying about it, examining his tools, but not
using them. He is therefore awkward in his use of
them. The child with perhaps fewer tools—a smaller
supply of available words, perhaps, for the first few
years—knows how to use them ; with his poorer tools
he is a more skillful worker. Mr. Yoshimura remarked in the course of his address here some days ago, that
to merely understand books is not true aim of language study, and that there is still a tendency among
students to limit the wide sphere of linguistic study to
the small compass of reading. He spoke the truth.

PROF. McKENZIE'S LECTURES.

There are four important points to observe in the study of English, namely, that the student should come to understand, speak, read, and write it. And to attain these ends, one must first master the familiar language of every day use. There are some parts of England where they are said to use only three or four hundred words. It is not a great number of difficult words so much as a small number of common words and phrases at his command that enables a man to speak expressively. Even Shakespeare, Milton or Macaulay could not have written their great works, had they not had as a foundation the colloquial language. In learning a foreign language, as in constructing a house, we must build up, and not down ; we must start at the foundation, not at the roof ; in other words we must go on from the easy language to the more difficult.

He then came to the Gouin System. Gouin, a Frenchman still living, went to Germany and there began to study the languge. He attempted in vain to master German with dictionaries and books of reference. He then went to live in a German family and studied German practically. In three months he attained such a mastery of the language that he could express himself readily in it. This led him to construct what is now commonly called the " Gouin System." His system aims at beginning the teaching of a foreign language at the point where the child begins, and starts with a series of short simple sentences, in the indicative mood and the present tense. To give a specimen :

  I *go* towards the door.   *go*

110 PROF. McKENZIE'S LECTURES.

I *come* to the door.   *come*

I *stand* before the door.   *stand*

It treats the verb as the most important word in the sentence.

Another effective system is Rosenthal's. It begins differently, giving a long complex sentence, at the beginning, and afterwards making an analysis of it, and thoroughly explaining it. The sentence given first in Rosenthal's French lessons is as follows:

"What do you want to do this afternoon? I should like to leave by the first train for Paris, but unfortunately that is impossible; for I expect a friend from Chicago, and must stay in Boulonge till the steamer arrives."

"This system is suitable, it seems to me," said Mr. McKenzie," for adults or somewhat advanced students, the former, for younger students or beginners. In both systems, grammar is treated as a subject of secondary importance, books on grammar being used only for reference. Of the ten little volumes in this set of Rosenthal, the grammar is *tenth*. Both aim at cultivating the ear, the tongue, the eye, and the hand. The one, as was said before, takes at first short sentences, which can be easily comprehended and memorized, and later on, longer and more complicated ones, compound and complex sentences replacing the simple ones. The other takes a long sentence and breaks it up into its component parts and thoroughly studies it.

CHAPTER II.

NATURAL METHOD.

Mr. McKenzie was to give practical lessons to a class of Middle School students of the third year, from his book of *Natural Method Exercises,* which are, as he stated, simply *Gouin System Series* with some slight modifications introduced by himself. In advance he made a few remarks on the Gouin and Rosenthal Systems, as a continuation of his last lecture. Both systems insist on the use of the imagination, the students realizing the things talked of, and applying the new language to them so frequently that they become able to think in the new language. One gets to apply the new word *directly* to the thing, not translating it. And this is an important and essential point in language study. Both systems have been thoroughly tested with excellent results. An English and a Japanese carpenter plane and saw differently, but the same end is reached by both. So with these two systems. To apply the Classic Method to modern languages is like trying to plane with a saw.

He had always been at a disadvantage in using the Gouin system, both in studying Japanese and in teaching English. When he studied Japanese by this method, he had to tell his teacher of Japanese how to teach him on the one hand; while in teaching English to his pupils, he had always had too few hours with them to do the best work. Nevertheless he had found the

112 PROF. McKENZIE'S LECTURES.

system work excellently so far as he had tested it. He mentioned four advantages accruing from the teaching of a foreign language by the Natural Method :—

1. We can get the *idiom* of the language, that is to say, the right words and the right order of the words as used in a given language, naturally and easily. Difficult words, like the articles and prepositions, are thus speedily and surely learned.

2. Exceptional forms are learned without our knowing or thinking of them as exceptions.

3. We have here an easy and natural way of learning the grammar (tense, mood, etc.)

4. Repeating words, phrases and sentences after the teacher, the student gets the "tune" of the language.

But let it be remembered that the best results presuppose full and correct knowledge of the language on the part of the teacher. So far not many of you have studied English by the methods which emphasize the necessity of training first of all the *ear* and the *tongue*. The *eye* and the *hand* have had undue attention, to the neglect of more important organs. The teacher who would teach by this method or other similar ones must pay particular attention to the pronunciation, the accent, the emphasis, the "tune" of the language. He must cultivate the *ear* and the *tongue* especially.

Then referring to the question of helping the teachers to improve themselves in practical English, he spoke as follows :

"The more I think of it, the more I am convinced of the necessity of opening such schools as this, in which

PROF. McKENZIE'S LECTURES. 113

the teachers of English can have the greatest possible amount of practice. I would suggest two things :

1. That the teachers become pupils in series lessons, reading, free conversation, phonetics, etc.
2. That instead of three weeks, the school should last some two months.

As to the practicability of such a plan, I cannot judge, but of its desirability I think there can be little doubt."

He then gave a language lesson to the boys, first explaining, not scientifically but practically, certain difficult vowel sounds, as :

ō   as in no (also as in bore)

ạ   as in call.

ă   as in cat, mat, man.

û   as in full(much mispronounced as ōō, as in fool).

He next directed the students (3rd year class) to open their books at page 57 (*Natural Method Exercises in Japanese and English*, prepared by himself), and taught a series of simple sentences, reading himself first, they repeating the sentences after him. I need scarcely say that strict attention was paid to pronunciation and accent. The lesson in question (which the boys were told to have by heart by the next hour fixed for this subject) was as follows :

28.—SAILING THE BOAT.

The mȯth'ẹr gĭveṣ hẽr boy ạ *toy [19]
                         ⌊*bōat. gives
Shē tĕllṣ hĭm tọ bē cȃre'fûl of
                         ⌊[ŏv] ĭt. tells...to be careful

114 PROF. McKENZIE'S LECTURES.

The boy tīeṣ ạ *strīng tọ thẹ *bow[20]

          ⌊of thẹ̣ boat. **ties**

Hē tākes thẹ boat to the *pŏnd.⸱ **takes**

He pûts the boat ĭn'tô the wạ'tẹr. **put...into**

The boat flōats *pĕr´fẹct-ly [*jŭst

          ⌊rīght]. **floats**

The boy wạlks ạ-lŏng´ the ĕdġe

          ⌊of the pond. **walks**

He pûllṣ the boat a-long´ ăft'ẹr him. **pulls**

The string cătch'ẹṣ ŏn ạ *rēed. **catches**

The boy trīeṣ to gét it ọff. **tries to get...off**

Bŭt he căn'nŏt dô sō. **cannot do so**

So he breāks the string. **breaks**

And ties the brō'ken ĕndṣ *tọ-

          ⌊gĕth'ẹr. **ties**

    The pages of the book opposite the English lessons are allotted to Japanese sentences corresponding to the English. He first read the Japanese and then the English.

CHAPTER III.

NATURAL METHOD.

The professor reviewed the boys (the third year class) on the lesson he had given them the previous day, first going over the verbs, and then asking them to give the sentences containing them. Strict examination was made of their pronunciation and accent, accurate illustration being given in the case of any difficult sound they failed to utter properly. After the boys had fairly acquainted themselves with the sentences, he proceeded to give them the next lesson by the same method as before, i. e. making them read after him. Below are given the sentences :

The boy *găth′ẹrṣ sȯme smạll
⌊stĭcks ănd *stōneṣ. **gathers**
He pûts thĕm ĭn′tô thẹ bōat. **puts...into**
He cạll̥ṣ them *eär′gō. **calls**
He pulls the boat a-long′ as bẹ-
⌊fōre.′ **pulls**
The boat strīkes *ạ-gaĭnst′ the
⌊*shōre. **strikes**
It tĭps tọ one [wŭn] sīde. **tips**
The car′go *slīdeṣ to thē edge. **slides**
The boat *eăp-sī′zeṣ. **capsizes**
The sticks go flōat′ịng ạ-wāy′. **go floating**
The stones *sink [sĭngk] to the
⌊bot′tọm. **sink**

116 PROF. McKENZIE'S LECTURES.

The boy pulls the boat out.   **pulls...out**

He takes the boat băck to the house.   **takes...back**

From the "Question Box" came several difficult questions, all by one teacher, which reflect credit upon him as a believer in the proverb "It is never too late to learn." Mr. McKenzie thoroughly explained them one by one, so that the questioner was made, I believe, a little wiser in the line of teaching English.

Ques. "What is the difference of meaning between the two sentences?"

'You are going, are you?'

'Are you going?'

Ans. "The former refers to something said before and has much the sense of : 'You have definitely decided to go, have you?' while the latter is simply a question asking one's intention of going, and nothing more."

Ques. "How to read '1.60 *yen*,' and '3.30 p.m.'?"

Ans. "'1.60 *yen*,' is read 'one yen and sixty sen,' or 'one yen, sixty sen,' or more commonly, 'one-sixty,' when the sense of 'dollar' or '*yen*' is definitely implied. '3.30 p.m.' is generally read 'half past three, in answer to the question 'What time is it?' or 'half past three in the afternoon' if one is referring to a time not present, i. e. past or future. But when applied to the railway time-table and in similar cases, it is read 'three-thirty p.m.,' or simply, 'three-thirty.'"

Ques. "What is the meaning of 'Bless my soul!'?"

PROF. McKENZIE'S LECTURES.

117

Ans. "It is an interjection used when something surprising has happened. 'Well, I declare!' is used in a similar case.

In accordance with a request of teachers Profs. Gauntlett and McKenzie taught them the national anthem of England, the one playing the organ, and the other accompanying him in the singing. The song is as follows :

GOD SAVE THE KING.

God save our gra-cious King,
1   1   2   7   1   2

Long live our noble King,
3   3   4   3 2   1

God save our King ;
2   1   7   1

Send him vic-tori-ous,
5   5   5   5 4 ⌊,3

Hap-py and glo-ri-ous,
4   4   4   4 3 2

Long to reign o-ver us ;
3   43 2 1 3 4 5

God save our King.
6 5 4   3   2   1

The two professors sang three or four times, followed by the teachers in a low unmusical voice. Then they sang in concert a popular song of the Welsh people. The song is given below :

MARCH OF THE MEN OF HARLECH.

Men of Harlech, march to glory,

Victory is hov'ring o'er ye,
Bright ey'd freedom stands before ye,
Hear ye not her call?
At your sloth she seems to wonder,
Rend the sluggish bonds asunder,
Let the war-cry's deaf'ning thunder,
   Every foe appal.

CHORUS.

Echoes loudly waking, hill and valley shaking,
Till the sound spreads wide around,
The Saxon's courage breaking;
Your foes on ev'ry side assailing,
Forward press with heart unfailing,
Till invaders learn with quailing,
   Cambria ne'er can yield.

CHAPTER IV.

NATURAL METHOD.

The method used was the same as that referred to previously. The professor asked the boys (3rd year class) to give the past tense of the verbs used in the sentences he had taught first.

QUESTIONS ANSWERED.

Quest. "Are there any colloquial English dictionaries?"

Ans. "None that I know of. Abbreviated dictionaries, such as Webster's pocket dictionary, necessarily contain the most familiar words, and therefore are largely colloquial.

Skeat's 'Etymological Dictionary' is recommended for the study of derivations."

Ques. "What books of reference are the best to use in studying Shakespeare, Milton, Scott, and Tennyson?"

Ans. "Rolfe's (Am. Book Co.,) and Deighton's (Macmillan) are good in studying Shakespeare. As to Milton, there are probably good books of reference, but I am not acquainted with them. As his works contain so many classical allusions a 'Dictionary of Classic Mythology' would be very useful. In studying the works of Scott and Tennyson, I am not able to refer you to any particular books. But pro-

PROF. McKENZIE'S LECTURES.

bably their poems, with notes, are published by such houses as Macmillan and Co. Such text books are prepared for High schools in America, and I have no doubt any you need can be obtained.

Ques. "Who are the most popular writers now in England and America?"

Ans. There are many, but the following are among the best known:

Tolstoi (Russian)—Many works translated into English.

Max 'ORell (French, but wrote in English. Lately deceased)—'John Bull and His Island.'

Conan Doyle (English)—Detective stories. His 'Sherlock Holmes' stories are well known.

Hall Caine—'The Eternal City.'

Mrs. Humphry Ward—'Eleanor.'

John Morley—'Life of Gladstone.'

Kipling—Poems.

Stockton—'Bar Harbor.'

Ralph Connor—'Black Rock.'

Marion Crawford (English).

Gilbert Parker (Canada, English).

Charles Dudley Warner (American).

Henry Van Dyke (American)—'Blue Flower.'

Ques. "What dictionaries are the most practical for studying phonetic marks?

Ans. "Century, Standard, Webster, Worcester."

Ques. "What Bible commentaries are the best?"

Ans. "Jameison, Fawcett and Brown's—(about 10 *yen*?)

Clarke's—(about 15 *yen*?)

Henry's—(about 15 *yen*?)

PROF. McKENZIE'S LECTURES.   121

Cambridge Bible—(50 *yen?*)

Expositor's Bible—(35 *yen?*)

There are many other good commentaries. Any information desired concerning such books can be obtained by applying to the Kyobunkwan, Ginza, 4 Chome, Tokyo."

Ques. "What is the best dictionary of synonyms?"

Ans. "Crabbe's was some years ago. It is good. There may be better now. Trench's 'Study of Words' is also very interesting and useful."

CHAPTER V.

NATURAL METHOD.

The method was the same as that referred to previously. The new lesson was as follows :

30.—COASTING.

Thẹ boy gĕts down hĭṣ ˟slĕd
⌊(*hănd′-slei*gh*). **gets down**
Hē pûl*l*ṣ, thẹ slĕd ạ-lŏng′ ō′vẹr thẹ
⌊snōw. **pulls**
He gōeṣ tô ạ *nei*gh*′bọr-ịng *hĭ*ll*. **goes**
He *clĭmb*ṣ to the tŏp ŏf the hill. **climbs**
He türnṣ the sled ạ-round′. **turns (trnz)**
He *points the frȯnt of the slĕd
⌊tōw′ạrdṣ the fôot of the hill. **points**
He sīts down ŏn the sled. **sits down**
He tākes hōld of the front of the
⌊sled. **takes hold**
He stĭcks one [wŭn] fôot out *bẹ-
⌊hīnd′ the sled. **sticks…out**
He pûsh′ẹ*th* the snow wĭth his foot. **pushes**
The sled stärts. **starts**
The sled goes *fȧst′ẹr and fast′er. **goes**
The boy *stēerṣ the sled with his
⌊foot. **steers**

PROF. McKENZIE'S LECTURES.   123

The sled gĕts nē*a*r the bŏt′t*o*m
         ⌊of the hill. **gets near**

The sled strīk*e*s ạ-gȧinst′ a lärġ*e*
         ⌊stōn*e*. **strikes**

The sled *ŭp-sĕts′.   **upsets**

The boy fạll*ṣ* ọ*ff*.   **falls off**

The boy goes rōl′l*i*ng ō′v*ẹ*r in snow. **goes rolling**(g ⊼ ᵥz)

At the bot′tom of the hill he stŏps. **stops**

He gets up.   **gets up**

He is not *hürt.   **is not hurt**

He climbs up to his sled.   **climbs up**

He turns the sled rī*g*ht sīd*e* ŭp. **turns**

He pulls the sled up to the top of
         ⌊the hill. **pulls...up**

He *cōạsts (rīd*e*ṣ) down the hill ạ
        ⌊′nŭm′b*ẹ*r of tīm*e*ṣ. **coasts (k⁻os** ꭹ**)**

When [hwĕn] he is tīr*e*d he goes
        ⌊bȧck *hōm*e*. **is...goes**

After the classes, the following song was sung by
Messrs. Gauntlett and McKenzie :

THE MIDSHIPMITE.

' T was in '55 on a winter's night, (sailors' cry)
We'd got the Russian lines in sight,
When up comes a little midshipmite, (sailors' cry)
" Who'll go ashore to-night " says he,
" And spike their guns along with me? "

124   PROF. McKENZIE'S LECTURES.

"Why bless ye, sir, come along," say we,
(Sailors' cry)

Chorus : With a long, long pull,
And a strong, strong pull,
Gaily boys make her go,
And we'll drink to-night
To the midshipmite,
Singing cheerily, lads, yo ho !

CHAPTER VI.

NATURAL METHOD.

The professor first had the boys of the third year Middle School class repeat the sentences he gave them the last day, as usual, and then questioned them on the first lesson (Sailing the Boat) changing many of the nouns into pronouns. The boys were also required to answer by using pronouns instead of nouns wherever practicable, and this they did, using their books to help their memories. It was evident that they were to get thorough mastery of the lesson by means of constant repetition and application. The questions and answers were written on the board, and copied by the boys. By this means they could, as the professor said, practise writing also, which was one of the aims of the method. The questions and answers which they had to memorize by the next day, were as follows:

Prof. "What did the mother give her boy?"

Stud. "She gave him a toy boat."

Prof. "What did she tell him?"

Stud. "See told him to be careful of it."

Prof. "Then what did the boy do?"

Stud. "He tied a string to the bow (of the boat)."

Prof. "Then what did he do with the boat?"

Stud. "He took it to the pond."

Prof. "Where did he put it?"

126 PROF. McKENZIE'S LECTURES.

Stud. "He put it into the water."

Prof. ".How did it act?"

Stud. "It floated perfectly."

Prof. "Where did the boy walk?"

Stud. "Along the edge of the pond." (elliptical form).

Prof. "What did he do with the boat?"

Stud. "He pulled it along after him." (This can hardly be further abbreviated).

Prof. "What happened as he pulled the boat along?"

Stud. "The string caught on a reed."

Prof. "What did the boy do?"

Stud. "He tried to get it off."

Prof. "Did he succeed?"

Stud. "No, he failed."

Prof. "Then what did he do?"

Stud. "He broke the string."

Prof. "And then?"

Stud. "He tied the broken ends together."

Many suggestions were made in pronunciation among which a few useful ones may be mentioned here: "Puts into" should be pronounced as "put-sin'-to."

Vocalize the "e" in "catches." It is an obscure vowel, but not quite silent. If pronounced "cat'-ches," this vowel sound will be clearer.

The "a" in "walk" is the same as "aw" in "caw," and "saw," in pronunciation. The "l" is silent.

"R" should not be pronounced with a strong trill.

To practice the sounds in the combinations "st" and "sts," the following lines were given:

PROF. McKENZIE'S LECTURES.

"Amidst the mists and coldest frosts,
With stoutest wrists and loudest boasts,
He thrusts his fists against the posts,
And still insists he sees the ghosts."

CHAPTER VII.

NATURAL METHOD.

The professor had the boys (3rd year Middle School class) repeat the last lesson, which was afterward recited in the Past Tense. He then remarked that if time were sufficient the sentences would be given in various Tenses, Persons, etc. as :

Ques. " What is the mother going to give her boy ? "

Ans. " She is going to give him a toy boat."

Ques. " What has the mother just given her boy ? "

Ans. " She has just given him a toy boat."

Ques. " What will the mother give her boy to-morrow ? "

Ans. " She will give him a toy boat (to-morrow)."

Ques. " What will you give the boy ? "

Ans. " I shall give him a toy boat."

Ques. " What did your mother give you ? "

Ans. " She gave me a toy boat."

Ques. " What did she tell you ? "

Ans. " She told me to be careful of it."

Ques. " Did your mother give you a sword ? "

Ans. " No, she gave me a toy boat."

Ques. " What was your mother giving you when I came in ? "

Ans. " She was giving me a toy boat (when you came in)."

PROF. McKENZIE'S LECTURES. 129

The professor further added that the simple sentences should also be combined into compound or complex sentences, where this could properly be done, and so the lesson be put into the form of a continuous narrative. The teacher should as far as possible give variety to the lesson. He should also lead his pupils from the known to the unknown. And in this work of foundation laying he would do well to take the maxim " Make haste slowly " as his motto.

CHAPTER VIII.

A STUDY IN THE ENGLISH POETS.

. After announcing certain changes in the programme, Prof. McKenzie entered upon his lecture. He said that it was a great pity to find a tendency among students of English to neglect the study of English poetry. What is the object of the study of English in Japan? Is it only for the sake of making Japan one of the greatest commercial nations in the world? This is no doubt one object, but not the only one. If it were merely for commercial purposes, the study of the English language might well be restricted to the students of commercial schools, to merchants, and to those intending to go abroad. The most important aim in studying the English language, is the understanding of the spirit of the Anglo-Saxon race, the source of its progress and power. Greek and Latin are studied in European countries for their culture and philosophy. To study a people we must study their literature, not the prose writings alone, but the poetry as well. The poet is the seer, who understands and voices the fears, hopes, aspirations of his people. In his writings we see the real national life as it is revealed nowhere else. And because his work is preserved in beautiful and moving language, it remains to please and instruct long after he has passed away. Japan will be better understood by the West when the West knows her poetry better, but

PROF. McKENZIE'S LECTURES. 131

at present that part of her literature is almost a sealed book to them.

"Your work," he said, "is largely elementary, but your own knowledge of English should be broad and deep. If you know the beauties of the literature you can inspire your pupils. You must read much more than you teach; in other words, you must have reserve force, and not 'have all your goods in the shop window.' Pupils will learn with confidence when they find that their teacher's knowledge is broad and deep. The knowlege imparted should be but a cupful out of a full bucket. Your studies should not be confined to the text-books you teach. The student of the classics never leaves out Homer or Virgil; so no student of English should leave out Shakespeare, Tennyson, etc. Poetry is more difficult to understand than prose, though more primitive. Macaulay spoke the truth when he said that 'as a nation becomes more philosophical, it becomes less poetical.' Poetry is the language of emotion and belongs to the childhood or youth of the nation. The greatest poets of Greece, Rome, Italy, and England, and of many other nations appeared in the earlier ages. In English, poetry forms the greater part of the early literature, one writer having gone so far as to remark that 'Early English literature is almost exclusively one of poetry.'"

Then coming to the question as to why poetry is more difficult than prose, he gave two or three main reasons :—

1. It abounds in figures of speech.
2. Many peculiar or unusual words are used.

132   PROF. McKENZIE'S LECTURES.

3. The order of the words is often different from that found in prose.

He next mentioned certain peculiarities in the order and in the words used in Poetry, as follows :—

I. Omissions.

(a) of Articles :

Like (a) shipwreck'd mariner on (a) desert coast.'

(b) of Antecedent :

(He) " Who never fasts no banquet e'er enjoys."

(c) of the introductory *there* :

(There) " Was no sight about but images of rest."

(d) of the Relative in the Nominative Case :

" For is there aught in sleep (which or that) can charm the wise ? "

II. Abbreviations are frequent :

Nouns : helm (for helment), morn (morning), consult (consultation) etc.

Adjectives :   dread(ful), lone(ly), yon(der),

Verbs :   list(en), ope(n), dark(en).

III. Strange and antiquated words :

Ire, ken, lore ; heapy, blithe, dank ; wilder (verb), doff, trow : inly, felly, starky : adown (preposition), aneath (preposition) aslant : hast, hath, wast : thy, thou, ye, etc.

IV. The order is inverted :

3   4   2   1   5   6   7
" No hive hast thou of horded sweets."

1   3   2   4   6   5
" Come, nymph demure, with mantle blue."

PROF. McKENZIE'S LECTURES. 133

1 2 3 4 6 7 8 9 5
"As oft as I to kiss the flood decline."

3 1 2 4 5 6 7
"Follow I must, I cannot go before."

5 6 7 3 4 1 2
"Against your fame with fondness hate combines."

9 1 2 3 6 7 8 4 5
"Part the fine locks her graceful head that deck."

V. Intransitive verbs are sometimes used as Transitives, and *vice versa:*

" Before I would have granted (= consented) to that act."

" To meditate (upon) the blue profound below."

The above are the most important divergences from the language and order found in prose.

CHAPTER XIV.

A STUDY IN THE ENGLISH POETS.

(CONCLUDED)

Mr. McKenzie kindly lent me the notes of his lecture, from which the following was rewritten with some slight changes.

"I spoke yesterday of the study of English literature in order to obtain a knowledge of the English people, to get an insight into the Anglo-Saxon character, to come to understand the hidden springs of the national life, and to have fellowship with the spirit of this race. But while this should be our chief aim in studying the literature of any people, and your aim in studying English literature, poetry included, there are advantages of a minor kind to be derived from the study of English poetry. To mention a few of them :

1. Poetry being written in regular measure, viz. with accents at definite intervals, and much of it being rhymed, i, e. having similar sounds recurring in regular order at the ends of lines, a constant study of poetic writings by the teacher, will, I believe, be a great help to him in his attempt to acquire a correct pronunciation. There is not absolute uniformity in the matter of accents and rhyme, but in some poems there is very little irregurality. Critical reading of prose and poetry will help the teacher to

PROF. McKENZIE'S LECTURES.   135

detect these irregularities. The variations in accent
are found mostly at the beginning of lines, as :

"Some' to the sun' their insect' wings' unfold,

Waft' on the breeze' or sink' in clouds' of

gold."—Pope.

To give a few lines in which the accent and rhyme
are both uniform :

"But now' secure' the painted vessel glides

The sunbeams trembling' on' the flowing tides."
                                                —Pope.

"The harp,' his sole' remaining joy'

Was carried by' an orphan boy."—Scott.

"For well-a-day, their date' was fled,

His tuneful brethren all' were dead."—Scott.

"I falter' where I firmly trod'

And falling with' my weight of cares'

Upon' the great world's altar stairs'

That slope' through darkness up' to God."
                                                —Tennyson.

There is much in the above three poets, and many
others, with is entirely regular both in rhyme and
accent. To read these will help you practically in
acquiring the "tune" of the language. Note that
the rhyme is correct throughout—glides, tides, joy,
boy etc., though God is often pronounced with a

136 PROF. McKENZIE'S LECTURES.

rather broader *o* sound than that found in *trod.*
From your books dealing with the rules governing
poetic writings you will learn the limits of license
allowed the poets in the matter of variations in
rhyme.

2. The study of poetry will enlarge your vocabulary, your stock of phrases, especially. Much that
the poets have written has entered into the warp
and woof of the language. The happiest turns of
thought have been seized upon, and made to do
service in the language of our every-day life. In
this way our ordinary conversation has been made
more elegant, less sordid, than it otherwise would
have been. For this enrichment of the language we
owe no small debt to our poets. I purpose giving you
some quotations from Shakespeare that are now in
familiar use. Shakespeare is so much studied that it
is easier to gather up such quotations from his writings. In the following list are found some of the
most common quotations from him. Had time permitted a number from other poets would have been
included.

QUOTATIONS FROM SHAKESPEARE.

As good luck would have it.
As merry as the day is long.
Good men and true.
All the world's a stage.
At my fingers' ends.
A word and ǀa blow.

PROF. McKENZIE'S LECTURES. 137

A man can die but once.
Every inch a king.
The better part of valour is discretion.
Be just, and fear not.
Brevity is the soul of wit.
Comparisons are odorous (odious).
Curses, not loud, but deep.
A custom more honoured in the breach than in
the observance.
Done to death.
The devil can cite (quote) scriptures.
To dance attendance on.
Hoist with his own petard.
For ever and a day.
Food for powder.
Good luck lies in odd numbers.
Give the devil his due.
Give me the ocular proof.
Home-keeping youth.
How the world wags.
He hath(has) eaten me out of house and home.
In single blessedness.
In maiden meditation, fancy free.
I know a trick worth two of that.
I have had my labour for my travail (pains).
It was Greek to me.
I have bought golden opinions.
I'll make assurance doubly sure.
I bear a charmed life.
In my mind's eye.
It out-Herod's Herod.
It means mischief.

PROF. McKENZIE'S LECTURES.

A towering passion.
More sinned against than sinning.
Nothing, if not critical.
It beggared all description.
Love is blind.
As true as steel.
My cake is dough.
Making night hideous.
Neither rhyme nor reason.
One touch of nature makes the whole world kin.
One may smile and smile and be a villain.
Observed of all observers.
That way madness lies.
Such stuff as dreams are made of.
A soul of goodness in things evil.
Something is rotten in the State of Denmark.
Suit the action to the word.
Sent to my account.
The king's English.
Thereby hangs a tale.
Tell truth and shame the devil.
Thy wish was father to that thought.
The course of true love never did run smooth.
Too much of a good thing.
The livelong day.
The most unkindest cut of all.
An itching palm.
Throw physic to the dogs.
That it should come to this !
To the manner born.
They fool me to the top of my bent.
'T'is neither here nor there.

PROF. McKENZIE'S LECTURES. 139

The game is up.
The very pink of courtesy.
What's mine is yours.
The whirligig of time.
The weakest goes to the wall.
What's in a name?
When shall we three meet again?
We have scotch'd the snake.
What man dare, I dare.
Die with the harness on.
While memory holds a seat.
Who steals my purse steals trash.

I purpose giving you a list of the most noted of the English poets—many who have written well are necessarily omitted—and indicate briefly their place in English literature. The description as well as the list, will necessarily be very imperfect, but may be an indication to you as to where you will find it most useful to delve. I shall follow, for the most part, the chronological order."

1. Chaucer (born in London 1328).

The first great English poet. "English poetry begins with Chaucer, the first skilled and conscious workman." * Antiquated forms make the study of his poems difficult. But English lovers of literature read him with delight. "His variety and power of diction not ten his successors have been able to rival." His

---

*Welsh, in *Development of English Literature and Language,* from which work I shall frequently quote.

140 PROF. McKENZIE'S LECTURES.

pupil Occleve said he was "The first finder of our fair language." "He rescued the native tongue from Babylonish confusion, and established a literary diction, banishing from Anglo-Saxon the superannuated and uncouth, and softening its churlish nature by the intermixture of words of Romance fancy." His best known poem is "Canterbury Tales."

2. Spenser (1552). His chief work is the "Fairie Queene," the best poetic allegory in the English language, as Bunyan's "Pilgrim's Progress" is the best prose allegory. Its aim was "to fashion a gentleman in virtuous and gentle discipline." Its somewhat antiquated style causes it to be less read than it deserves.

3. Shakespeare (1564). With Shakespeare we get fairly into *modern* English, though some remnants of the older forms are still seen. As Emerson says of Plato, "I am struck, in reading him, with the extreme modernness of his style and spirit," so we may say of Shakespeare. As one critic has said, "His thoughts, passions, feelings, strains of fancy, all are of this day as they were of his own ; and his genius may be contemporary with the mind of every generation for a thousand years to come." Many lines or phrases of his are now common property—a part of the vocabulary of every educated person and in some cases of the uneducated also. People use Shakespeare's phrases without knowing whence they come. His language is largely Anglo-Saxon, and idiomatic. He excels in all directions, in tragedy and comedy, in song and sonnet. "To excel in pathos, in wit or in humor, in sublimity, as

Milton, in intensity, as Chaucer, or in remoteness, as Spenser, would form a great poet, but to unite all, as he has done is, ' To get the start of the Majestic world, and bear the palm alone,' " His characters live and breathe. We know them as well as we do our contemporaries in the flesh. Of such are Hamlet, Lear, Falstaff, Juliet, Rosalind, Shylock, Othello. But in your reading of Shakespeare you need to remember that he reflects the manners of the age in which he lived. Manners and morals have improved since his time, and there are passages which would not be tolerated in public to-day, which evidently gave no offence in his day. This is especially true in regard to the relation of the sexes. A lady reader of Shakespeare, Mrs. Scott Siddons, I think it was, gave readings from Shakespeare's writings some years ago in the United States, and a gentleman who heard her says, " She skipped from point to point in a way that reminded one of a person crossing a brook by jumping from stone to stone." We do not blame Shakespeare for such unreadable passages. He no doubt truly mirrored the age in which he lived. The present day audience is more refined, and consequently more particular about what it hears. But these passages form only a small portion of the whole of Shakespeare. We may pass over them all, and not lose anything of value, or much in quantity. Shakespeare was called by some of his contemporaries, the " Honey-tongued," to show their appreciation of his musical lines. " His versification is powerful, sweet, and varied, naturally and enduringly musical." His is the largest vocabulary of any English

142 PROF. McKENZIE'S LECTURES.

writer—estimated at 12,000 words (Milton 11,000, Carlyle 9,000). Some of the favorites among his works are "Hamlet," "Macbeth," "Henry IV," "Midsummer Night's Dream," "Much Ado about Nothing."

4. Milton (1608). "The most sublime of all the English poets." His greatest work is "Paradise Lost." But there are others of a lighter kind, very musical and beautiful, for example, "Comus," "L'Allegro," and "Il Penseroso." The chief difficulty in reading Milton is to understand his numerous references to classic history and literature.

5. Pope (1688). "He made correctness his aim." "Refined, graceful, musical." "A poet of the second order." His greatest work is the "Essay on Man."

6. Burns (1759). "By far the greatest peasant poet that has ever appeared." Difficult for foreigners, because mostly in Scotch dialect. Among his best known poems are : "Cotter's Saturday Night," "Tam O'Shanter," "To a Mountain Daisy."

7. Cowper (1731). "The Task," "John Gilpin."

8. Goldsmith (1728). "Deserted Village."

9. Coleridge (1772). "The Ancient Mariner."

10. Scott (1771). Picturesque. Strong in simple narrative. Best known poems : "Lady of the Lake," "Lay of the Last Minstrel."

11. Wordsworth (1770). Writes in simple and graceful language. "The Excursion" is his great work.

12. Byron (1788). "The Revolutionary Poet." Individualistic—not universal. False ideals, capricious tastes. Great poetic power, but for above reasons not so much read as some other poets in this list. Great work : "Harold."

PROF. McKENZIE'S LECTURES. 143

13. Browning (1812). Like Carlyle in prose, difficult.

14. Whittier (1807). The Quaker Poet. One of the best known and most read of American poets.

15. Longfellow (1807). "The central figure of American poetry. The poet of daily life, familiar experience and domestic affection." Chief works : "Hiawatha" and "Evangeline."

16. Tennyson (1810). "A born artist, a master of charm, a lover of form and color... an ethical instructor." "Novel and despised first, he has become a classic in his own life time*...The representative of our refined, speculative and composite age." Noted works : "Idylls of the King," "Princess," "In Memoriam."

---

* Tennyson died a few years ago.

CHAPTER XV.

ENGLISH PROSE WRITERS.

In studying English literature, it is of course very important for us to acquaint ourselves with modern prose writers in order to follow the current thoughts and affairs of England and America. But we must not neglect old writers for all that. There are, it is true, many noted writers to-day, some writing articles for newspapers, or for magazines, and others writing good fiction or books dealing with present day affairs. But as there is a greater demand for books now than there was in former times, many of the authors now write under pressure, to satisfy the demand of the reading public. Much of the literary work of to-day is, therefore, less finished than that of earlier writers, who did their work in a more leisurely and careful manner. Under such circumstances, we must look rather to the latter for a good, pure style, than to the former. The professor then proceeded to give a list of the most famous English prose writers especially from the Elizabethan age down to the present, making critical remarks concerning each.

ENGLISH PROSE WRITERS.

1. Wycliffe(born 1324). "Established a sacred dialect which with slight variations continues to this day." His monumental work is the translation of the Bible into English. It has since been re-translated, but much of it remains practically where Wycliffe

PROF. McKENZIE'S LECTURES.   145

left it. He was the English reformer. By his translation of the Bible he did a great work in fixing the forms of the English language.

2. Bacon (1561). "The principal figure in English prose." He was born three years before Shakespeare. The two are the best representatives of the Elizabethan age in prose and poetry respectively. His style is "clear, strong, elaborate." His *Essays* are what live. "Few books are more quoted; few are more generally read."

3. Bunyan (1628). Simple, idiomatic. His great work is "Pilgrim's Progress," the noblest allegory in the English tongue. It is said that 93% of the words used in it are Anglo-Saxon.

4. De Foe (1661). Simple, vigorous, idiomatic. His best known work is "Robinson Crusoe."

5. Addison (1672). "Graceful, vivid, elegant. A model of pure and elegant English." "Vision of Mirza," "Immotality of the Soul," and "Sir Roger de Coverly," are among his best known writings.

6. Johnson (1709). "Heavy, antithetical, rolling, pompous." He loved words derived from Latin. "Lives of the Poets" is his greatest work. "Rasselas" is also well known. His was the first real English Dictionary.

7. Goldsmith (1728). "The most charming and versatile writer of the 18th century." "Vicar of Wakefield" is his best known prose work.

8. Scott (1771). "Easy, graceful, graphic." "Ivanhoe" is one of the best known of his novels.

9. Lamb (1775). "Essays of Elia," "Tales from Shakespeare."

146 PROF. McKENZIE'S LECTURES.

10. Irving (1783). "What author has succeeded as well as he in making literature delicious?" "Sketch Book" and "Rip Van Winkle" are noted works of his.

11. Carlyle (1795). "A style of his own, new and strange, vivid, rugged, forceful." "Sartor Resartus," "Heroes and Hero Worship," "Essays."

12. Macaulay (1800). "Opulence of illustration and adornment, antithesis of ideas, regular sequence of thought, harmonious construction, incomparable lucidity." "Always correct English." A lover of the Classics, Latin and Greek. "Not satisfied till every paragraph concluded with a telling sentence, and every sentence flowed like running water." "The best story-teller in the language." Essays (Temple, the younger Pitt and Milton are among the best), "History of England."

13. Emerson (1803). American. "Refined, subtle, compact, epigrammatic." Wrote some poetry of a high order. His "Essays" (e. g. Representative Men) are characteristic.

14. Hawthorne (1804). Delighted in the wierd. "More elegant English was never written." The "Scarlet Letter" is one of his well known works.

15. Dickens (1809). Idiomatic and forceful. "David Copperfield," "Nicholas Nickleby," "Pickwick Papers," are among his best known books.

16. Ruskin (1819). "The greatest living master of English prose," said a critic twenty years ago. Ruskin died a few years since. "Mornings in Florence" "Seven Lamps of Architecture," and "Ethics of the Dust," are good examples of his style.

CHAPTER XVI.

THE SUBJUNCTIVE MOOD.

"I need not waste time," said the professor, "in telling you what the Subjunctive Mood is, for you all know that. The question is not 'What forms may be included under the Subjunctive Mood?' but 'What Subjunctive forms are proper to use at the present time?' I shall not discuss at length the number of the tenses of the Subjunctive Mood. Let it suffice to say that some (Brown and others) say it has two—present and past ; some (e. g. Bain) three —present, past, and future ; others (e. g. Maxwell) six, namely, present, present prefect, past, past perfect, future, and future perfect.

I shall first call your attention to such expressions as : —

"If I *shall have gone* { when / before } you arrive, please follow me."

"If I *will* go to Tokyo, I shall give myself pleasure of calling on you." The first of the forms given above is correct so far as grammar is concerned, but is rarely used. In fact I myself seldom or never use it or hear it used. The second is not good English. The import of the first is commonly conveyed by such idiomatic forms as that given below :

"If I happen to be gone (or, If I should be gone) when you get there, please follow me."

148 PROF. McKENZIE'S LECTURES.

Again, instead of "If I *will* go..." we say, "If I go......"

Your grammars tell you that "The Subjunctive forms are retained in the verb 'to be' to a larger extent than in other verbs." This is true. They also tell you that the tendency is to drop the peculiar forms of the Subjunctive Mood and substitute for them the Indicative forms. That too is true. Why did the Subjunctive Mood fall into disuse? Probably because so few Subjunctive forms in ordinary verbs (other than 'to be') are different from the Indicative (see outline conjugation).

Do not confuse the conditional form of the Indicative with the Subjunctive. It is superflous to tell you that the meaning of the one is different from that of the other, as:

1. 'If he were here, I should tell him.' (Sub.—supposition implied).

2. 'If he was here, (as you say he was) why did he not come to see me?' (Ind.—actuality indicated).

In earlier English there were no inflections for the Subjunctive. The root form was used all through, as:

PRESENT.

If I be	If we be
If thou be	If you be
If he (she, it) be	If they be

But about Shakespeare's time, the 2nd person, singular, underwent modification, the 2nd sing. Ind. being substituted for it, as: If thou *art*, (*knowest, etc.*) for If thou *be* (*know*, etc.).

PROF. McKENZIE'S LECTURES.   149

If thou *wert*, for, If thou *were*.
"This was the first step in the degradation of the Subjunctive," says one grammarian. There is a difference now between the use of the Subjunctive in literary English and in colloquial English. By *colloquial* (col = together, loquor = to speak) I mean the language of everyday life, whether spoken or written. The best writers will largely determine for us the proper forms to be used in both literary and colloquial English, though the usage of educated people will also have much to do in deciding the proper colloquial form. Remember that it is the leading authors that determine for the most part the use of language, and not the grammarians. Remember also that language was made first and grammar afterwards, and that we must not therefore follow grammarians, who are not always necessarily literati of rank, if their rules are not in harmony with the best usage.

I have arranged a paradigm which perhaps may help you somewhat."

R (Ruskin)
E (Emerson)   SUBJUNCTIVE MOOD.
M (Macaulay)

	TO BE	
	Literary.	Colloquial.
Pres. Sing. 1st	*If I be* If I be not ˑmistaken. . .	*If I am* If I am not mistaken. . .
2nd	*If thou be* (or, art) Languˑge of prayer and devotion, or in lofty or formal style.	(2nd plural is used, which see.)

PROF. McKENZIE'S LECTURES.

3rd	*If he, it* etc. *be* ... "especially if it *be* disposed." (R) "Ask the great man if there *be* none greater." (E) "If he that inquires *be* a holy soul" (E) "If this *be* just and right .." (R) "If it *be*, what will you gain?" (R) If it *rain*.	*If he, it* etc. *is* "If there *is* one artist more than another...(R) ...at least if the day *is* fine. (R) ...a child can grasp if it *is* intersted. (R) "If there *is* love between us...if not...(E) If it *rains*.
	NOTE :—We may instead of the last form above say : "If it should rain" and "If he should go" etc., though the use of "should" suggests a shade more of doubt.	
Pres. Plural. 1st	*If we be* If we *be* not there &c.	*If we are* If we *are* not there do not wait.
	NOTE :—But we may say, "If we *should not be* there in time" "If we *do not get* there in time."	
2nd	*If you be* If you *be* tired, rest.	*If you are* If you *are* tired, rest. "Now if you *are* interested."...(R)
3rd	·*If they be* "If they *be* beggars". ..(E)	*If they are* If they *are* beggars send them away. But we may say : If they *should be* beggars, or, If they *seem to be* beggars.
Past. Sing. 1st	*If I were* "If I *were* merely to treat of battles"(M)	*If I were* If I *were* in your place. "If I *was*" is decidedly vulgar in a supposition, though allowed in the indicative: If I *was* there (as you say I was) why did you not see me?
2nd	*If thou were*. Unusual. In devotional language replaced by Indicative "*If thou wert.*"	The plural "*If you were*" is used.

PROF. McKENZIE'S LECTURES. 151

3rd	*If he, it* etc. *were* " If it *were* also a subject interesting to yourself " (R) " If there *were* any magnet.. that would point.. .''(E)	*If he, it &c were* If he *were* here you could ask him. *If he was* is not good in a supposition, though not unfrequently heard.
Past. Plural.	Same as Indicative	Same as Indicative
Perfect.	Same as Indicative except that 3rd person *If he have been,* is used.	*If he has been.* If anything *has been* restored.'' (R)
Pluperfect.	Same as Indicative	
Futures.	*If I will go,* is not good English. *If you will go If he will go* etc. are all right. But in any case like Indicative. But "will" here seems to be the principal verb.	

Other Verbs.

"If he *go* into the factory." (E) "If he *have* but courage." (E) (If he *should go* into the factory.)	"If he ever *looks* down from the scaffold." (R) (If he *should look* down from the scaffold.)

Besides the 3rd Sing. Pres., only the 2nd Sing "thou" is implicated.

CHAPTER XVII.

"SHALL" AND "WILL"

"Not one Englishman in a hundred," says Macaulay, "knows the rules for the use of *shall* and *will* ; but not one in a hundred ever makes a mistake in using them." The first part of this statement is perhaps true, but the second is more difficult to believe, especially, if the Scotch and Irish are included. For these latter often misuse the words. Bain in his grammar tells of an Irishman who had fallen into the water and was in danger of drowning, when he cried out :

(1) "I *will* drown, and no one *shall* help me."

This literally means :

"I am determined to drown, and I will allow no one to help me."

What he really meant was :

"I am in danger of drowning and there is no one who will help me."

So the sentence should be :

"I shall drown, and no one will help me."

Even Goldsmith is guilty of a slip in this respect, perhaps because he was an Irishman, for he says :

(2) "If I draw a catgut to a great length, I *will* make it smaller than before."

Of course, instead of *will* he should have used *shall*.

(6) "And, if I die, no man *shall* pity me."

Shak. Rich. III.

PROF. McKENZIE'S LECTURES.   153

The predictive sense is here intended, and we should now use *will* and not *shall* in such a case.

(7) "They *shall* be apprehended by and by."

Shak. Henry V.

From the context we should now expect *will*; though in the same construction we might have *shall*, with the meaning "I guarantee their apprehension." The meaning is indicated by the context.

(8) "Fear not my lord, your servant *shall* do so."   Shak.

This is evidently a *promise*; so we should now have *will*.

The objectionable character of *shall* in certain circumstances, is indicated in a passage of Shakespeare's "Coriolanus":

(9) "Mark you his absolute *shall*."

The use of *shall* and *will*, however, even in Shakespeare's time, was changing, and we find also in his writings examples that are in strict accordance with the best present day usage. (See No. 11)

The following list was then given:

"SHALL" AND "WILL."

I. *Peculiar or Ancient Uses.*

1. "I *will* (shall) drown, and no one *shall* (will) help me." (wrong).

2. "If I draw a catgut to a great length, I *will* (shall) make it smaller than before" (wrong).

3. "I *will*(shall)be obliged to you."⎫ Used by Scotch
"We *will* (shall) be compelled."⎬ and Irish, but
                                                              ⎭ wrong.

154 PROF. McKENZIE'S LECTURES.

4. "If you much note him you *shall* (will) offend him." —Macbeth.

5. "My country *shall* (will) have more vices than it had before." —Macbeth.

6. "And, if I die, no man *shall* (will) pity me." —Rich. III.

7. "They *shall* (will) be apprehended by and by." —Henry V.

8. "Fear not my lord, your servant (=I) *shall* (will) do so." —Shak.

9. "Mark you his absolute *shall*." —Cor.

10. "Perhaps I *will* (shall?) return." —Shak.

11. "The spirit of my father grows strong within me, and I *will* no longer endure it... He that escapes me without some broken limb *shall* acquit him well... Charles, I thank thee for thy love to me, which thou *shalt* find I *will* most kindly requite... Truly, when he dies, thou *shalt* be his heir, for what he has taken away from thy father perforce, I *will* render thee again in affection ; by mine honour I *will*." (correct).

Shak. "As You Like It."

II. *Present-day Use.*

12. 1st Sing. *I will go.* (=I promise to go).
    I shall go. (predictive, i. e., simple futurity)

    Plural. *We will go.* ⎫ Same force as in Sing.
    We shall go. ⎭

13. 2nd Sing. *You will go.* ⎰a) Simple futurity.
    ⎱b) Polite form of command.

PROF. McKENZIE'S LECTURES.   155

Examples: a) "You will reach Kōbe at 10 o'clock." (Simple prediction. The *time-table* states it).

"You will not be molested on the way." (There is no danger of molestation).

b) "John, you will take this parcel to Mr. Smith." (Polite command).

"The regiment will encamp at the foot of the hill." (Commanding officer's order).

You shall go. (Something done because of the authority or power of the speaker).

Examples: "You shall go to school to-day." (Whether you wish to go or not. *I will* it).

"You shall see." (I will cause you to see.)

"You shall not be molested by the way." (I guarantee you against molestation).

14. 3rd Sing. *He will go* { a) Simple futurity.
b) Purpose on the part of the subject.

a) "He will go, though he does not wish to do so."

b) "He will go, I cannot prevent it."

He shall go. (Will of speaker. *I* so determine.) *Interrogative.*

15. 1st Sing. *Will I go?* Not a good form unless in an ironical sense.

Examples: "Will you go there to-morrow?" "Will I go? Well, I should say not."

Children and also grown-ups make the mistake of using this form for "Shall I go?" Probably the Irish and Scotch make the mistake most frequently. In America it is often heard.

Shall I go? (Is it your will that I go?

156   PROF. McKENZIE'S LECTURES.

16. 2nd Sing.   *Will you go?* (Is it your wish or
will to go?)
Shall you go? |Simple futurity.
Will you go? |
Bain says, *"Will"* is admissible, but
"shall" is preferable.

17. 3rd Sing.   *Will he go?* (Is he determined or
willing to go?)
Shall he go? (Is it your wish or
will?)

The Plural follows the analogy of the Singular.

III.   *Examples from Literature.*

18. "I *shall* cheerfully bear the reproach."   (M)

19. "Henceforth I *shall* speak of him as the
painter."   (R)

20. ... "as I *will* show you to-morrow."

21. ... "I *will* see that through."...

22. "*I'll* put a stone at my place."

23. "We *shall* find... more than truth..."

24. "And *shall* we have to learn them all?"

25. "We *will* trace its complete character."

26. "We *will* (*shall?*) quit the cathedral by the
western door."

27. "We *will* try to write it down."

28. "We *will* hope for the best."

29. "We *will* believe anything when you say we
ought."

30. ... "Opera glasses, with which you *shall* for
once ... see an *opus*"

31. You *shall* see things as they are."

PROF. McKENZIE'S LECTURES. 157

32. "You *shall* make diamonds of yourselves." (It is *my* wish).

33. "You *will* return home with a general impression.

34. "You *will* see a scholar's rude imitation."

35. "You *will* also please take it on my word."

36. "What *will* you gain by unpersonifying it?"

37. "You *will* see more of it to-morrow."

38. "He *will* try if he cannot explain."

39. "This *will* never do."

40. "It *will* be of little interest."

41. "Two critics *will* contradict each other."

42. "They *will* be against you."

QUESTIONS.

Ques. "Many grammarians do not include the Potential Mood among the Moods. Is it important to keep the mood?"

Ans. "You need not trouble yourselves much about the Potential Mood. "May," "can," "must," "might," "could," "would" and "should," become sometimes subjunctive and sometimes indicative, according to their use. It is evidently not necessary to keep the mood as an independent one since many good grammarians have discarded it. In any case follow the best grammars. It is only a question of definition. The language remains the same."

Ques. "How are the following to be read?"

1. Fox's tail.   2. Horses' tails.

158　　　PROF. McKENZIE'S LECTURES.

3. Horse's tail.　　　4. Fritz's basket.
5. Royal.　　　　　　6. Towel.

Ans. " 'Fox's tail,' as 'foxes tail' (e obscure, i.e. very weak in sound).

'Horses' tail's ⎰first word same in pronunciation
'Horse's tail' ⎱ in both cases.

'Fritz's basket,' as 'Frit'-zeṣ basket' (e is the same in sound here as in 'foxes')

'Royal' as Ṛạēạl ('oy' is the same in sound here as in 'boy,' and a in the second syllable is obscure).

'Towel' as ⱬ ⱴ'el. (e obscure, i.e. weak)."

Ques. "What is meant by 'half a kingdom'?"

Ans. " 'Half a kingdom' = a large tract or territory, supposed for convenience to be as large as half a kingdom."

After the classes Frof. Gauntlett gave us a few specimens of college and popular songs. It was very interesting to hear him sing the songs, now high, now low, now slow, now fast.

THE COBBLER AND THE CROW.

(A college song)

1.

There was a merry cobbler, busy as a bee,
Lī'ly, lĭ'ly, lĭ'ly, lĭ'ly, lī'— do—.
When an old black crow came and perched upon
　　a tree ; With his qua ! qua ! qua ! qua !
Lī'ly, lĭ'ly, lĭ'ly, lĭ'ly, lī'— do.

PROF. McKNEZIE'S LECTURES. 159

2.

Now wife you go and fetch my good old blunderbuss,
Lĭ'ly, lĭ'ly, lĭ'ly, lĭ'ly, lĭ'— do—
And I'll shoot yon crow for so much annoying us,
With his qua! qua! qua! qua!
Lĭ'ly, lĭ'ly, lĭ'ly, lĭ'ly, lĭ'—ᵴ do.

3.

The cobbler miss'd his aim, to hit the crow did
fail, Lĭ'ly, lĭ'ly, lĭ ly, lĭ ly, lĭ' do—,
But he shot his poor donkey right through the head
and tail, With his qua! qua! qua! qua!
Lĭ'ly, lĭ'ly, lĭ'ly, lĭ ly, lĭ'—do.

4.

The cobbler could not shoot, no, not to save his life ;
Lĭ'ly, lĭ'ly, lĭ'ly, lĭ'ly, lĭ'—do—.
He tried to shoot the crow, but he shot his darling
wife. With his qua! qua! qua! qua!
Lĭ'ly, lĭ'ly, lĭ'ly lĭ'ly, lĭ'—do.

5.

Now, having shot his wife, it filled his heart with
woe ; Lĭ'ly, lĭ'ly, lĭ'ly, lĭ'ly, lĭ'—do—.
So the cobbler shot himself because he couldn't
shoot the crow, With his qua! qua! qua! qua!
Lĭ'ly, lĭ'ly, lĭ'ly, lĭ'ly lĭ—do.

THE SKIPPERS OF ST. IVES.

(A popular song)

1.

'Twas on a Monday morning
As I came through St. Ives ;

PROF. McKENZIE'S LECTURES.

There were four and twenty skippers,
And four and twenty wives ;
And each wife she would be talking,
Each wife she would be heard,
" It seems to me," said Jack, said he
" We can't get in a word,"
" Clackety clack," said Will to Jack,
" Clackety clack," said he,
Folks say out there live mermaids be !
Say, boys, shall we go out to see ?

2.

So these four and twenty skippers,
Stole off most quietly,
And courted those fair maidens,
At the bottom of the sea,
And when they had courted gaily,
For a thousand years or so,
They remembered their wives, in Old St. Ives,
And thought it was time to go.
" Clackety-clack " &c.

CHAPTER XVIII.

THE RELATIVES "THAT" AND "WHICH."

"Whatever rule may be laid down for the Elizabethan use of the three relative forms (*who, which* and *that*) will be found to have many exceptions. Originally *that* was the only relative, and if Wycliffe's version of the New Testament be compared with that of 1611 it will be found that *which* and *who* largely replace in the latter the relative *that*."

"In Shakespeare's time there was great diversity. Later there was a reaction against *which* and *who*, for *that* had a smoother sound. Addison plead for a larger use of *who* and *which* in a humorous piece entitled 'The Humble Petition of Which and Who.' He makes the two Relatives say, 'We are descended from ancient families, and kept up our dignity till the jack-sprat *That* supplanted us.' Since Addison's time there has been a reaction against the too great use of *that*, and we have returned somewhat to the Elizabethan usage." (Abbott, in *Shakespearian Grammar*.)

From the above we see that constant change in regard to the use of these words has been going on, and we ought not therefore to wonder if at the present time there is some confusion in regard to the use of *which* and *that*. I have given 34 examples from Macaulay, and these show how completely he has reinstated *which* in the position of leading re-

162   PROF. McKENZIE'S LECTURES.

lative. Macaulay uses *which* unless there is some definite necessity for *that,* as, for example, after a superlative adjective, (see No. 21 where after *any* we might have expected *that*). The grammars say that *which* is to be used as the co-ordinate relative and *that* as the restrictive, as :

Please call the man *that* is in the garden. (restrictive) He gave me a dog, *which* (=and it) is in the garden. (co-ordinate) Macaulay altogether ignores this principle. According to this rule we should have *that* 38 times, and *which* 4 times, whereas we really have *which* 40 times and *that* twice. I cannot say whether Macaulay is consistent in this use of *which* in all his writings, but I imagine he is—at least in the later ones. The examples taken are from the first part of his '*History of England,*' written in the latter part of his life. I quoted a critic the other day who side, 'Macaulay always wrote correct English.' If so, which is right? Macaulay or the grammarians? Scott (35-70) is less particular than Macaulay about the details of his composition. He aimed more at large general effects. We accordingly find in his writings some inconsistencies. In No. 41 he actually uses *that* as a co-ordinate, which is hardly admissable. In No. 44 *that* is a restrictive. In No. 52 we might have expected *that* for euphony's sake, in "the dialogue *which* they maintained," as another *which* occurs later. In No. 60 there is a good reason for *which*—it follows *that.* In No. 61 we might have expected *that* after *all* ; though the sound is not bad, since the two words are separated by 'the glory.' Were these omitted, we ought rather to have *all that.*

PROF. McKENZIE'S LECTURES.   163

In No. 63 the second relative seems to be *that* for
euphony's sake. No. 65 may be regarded as a quotation. It is a form fixed in common use. This fact
in itself in would be sufficient, perhaps, to account
for *that*. No. 67 and 68 have *that* probably for the
reason that at the period Scott was describing *that*
was the usual or only relative. We may say, in a
word, that Scott seems entirely regardless of the
grammatical rule noticed above.

Ruskin is more careful than Scott. We do not see
any examples in this list in which *that* is used to
introduce a co-ordinate clause. But why in No. 79
'the years *that* approach,' and in No. 81 'the art
which so disposes'? Both are similar in construction.
I am inclined to think that *euphony* has much to do
with Ruskin's choice of relatives. Certainly he does
not recognize the grammatical rule on this point. In
the 21 sentences quoted he uses *which* at least 10
times to introduce a restrictive clause.

Irving : In No. 99 he seems to use *that* in introducing a co-ordinate clause. But in 93, 95, 100, and
105, we have *which* used in introducing restrictive
clauses. In the case of 93, however, a *that* precedes.

Emerson : We might expect *that* in 111, after the
superlative 'the most determined aim.' After *any* in
121 *that* seems in place. But in 110, 112, 116 and in
the beginning of 117, *which* is used restrictively. In
118 and 119, after *all*, we might have expected *that*.

Salisbury: A statesman. But before entering politics he was a journalist, and is a user of good English.
He, like Macaulay, uses *which* (at least in the examples
quoted) unless there is some reason rendering *that*

164 PROF. McKENZIE'S LECTURES.

clearly desirable, as in 131, 136 and 139, where *all*, *nothing* and *any* respectively precede the relative.

Rosebery : Also a scholar and an author. Most of the cases in which he uses *that* are similar to those referred to in the quotations from Salisbury. Notice 152, 153, 163 and 169.

The *that* used by Rosebery in 150 and in 155 seems to have been used for euphony's sake, or by chance. He is not so careful as Macaulay and Salisbury, but like them, he often uses *which* in a restrictive sense.

Balfour : We should expect *that* in 175. He uses *which* both as a restrictive and as a co-ordinate.

Morley : (182-190) Also uses *which* in both cases.

Cleveland (a noted lawyer before he was President): He had much experience in the exact use of language. In 196 *that* is apparently used for euphony's sake. In 202 *that* after *any* is good. But Cleveland seems to follow no definite rule of selection. He seems to take whichever comes first. Certainly he does not follow the grammars.

Milton : In 212 *which* is used after *this*, and is therefore in agreement with good present day usage. *That* would not be euphonious here. In 218 we have *which*, because *that* precedes. In 222 we have *no* ... *that* which accords with present day usage. In 224 the Nominative Case Relative is omitted. This is not according to good usage to-day, except in poetry. In 225 and 229 we have *that which* : we could not say *that that*. In 233 *that* follows a superlative, which is also what is required to-day. In 234 we have *all that*, as we might expect. But Milton uses *which* both as a restrictive and as a co-ordinate relative.

PROF. McKENZIE'S LECTURES.   165

See 211, 215, 221, 223, 230, 235, 236, where *which* is used in a restrictive sense.

Addison : Addison observed the usage of his day, using *that* by preference for restrictive clauses. Consequently in 241 we should have expected *that* after *all*, as in 242. Probably in 243 *which* is used in order to avoid using *that* twice, the latter relative *that* being used for *who*. In 244 and 245 *which* is evidently used because *that* precedes. Hence Addison is nearer in his use to the grammars than any of the others from whom examples have been taken. Nevertheless he was a champion of *"who"* and *"which,"* and desired that they should be more largely used.

To sum up, in the 250 examples given, *which* is used over 200 times, and *that* about 60 times. If the writers had followed the rules laid down in the grammars strictly, we should have expected many co-ordinate clauses, and few restrictive ones. What is the fact? We have fewer than 50 co-ordinate, and over 200 restrictive clauses. *Which*, therefore, is used to introduce some 150 restrictive clauses, i, e. twice or three times as often as *that* is used for the same purpose. We must therefore take the rule of the grammars that *which* is to be used in co-ordinate clauses, and *that* in restrictive, with reserve.

There are certain things which we may learn from a consideration of these examples :

1. That after a superlative adjective we should use *that*. (See No. 7.)

2. That after certain words having somewhat the force of the superlative we should do well to use *that*;

166   PROF. McKENZIE'S LECTURES.

nomely, after such words as *any, all, no, nothing,* etc. (See 88, 123, 139, 163.)

3. When *that* precedes, especially when it is the antecedent and comes immediately before the relative, we should use *which.* (See 69.)

4. *That* is used in certain fixed forms, quotations, etc. as in 65, 67, 85, 6, 7.

5. For co-ordinate always use *which* in spite of Scott's use of *that*, as in 41, and Irving's, as in 99.

6. The relative in the Objective Case is often omitted. The relative in the Nominative Case should *not* be, as it is in 224. In regard to the omission of the relative in the Objective, clearness and euphony must guide.

7. It is sometimes difficult to determine whether the clause is co-ordinate or restrictive. (See 99, 134, 214, 250.) Sometimes we may indicate whether the clause is restrictive or co-ordinate by the omission or use of a comma. There are, however, comparatively few of these ambiguous clauses.

8. *That* will be found more common in *colloquial* use, probably, than in literary. Bain implies this in what he says concerning the use of these two relatives.

9. Study the best writers ; consider the question of euphony in making your choice : do not use *that* as a co-ordinate : and remember that *that* is *never wrong* used a restrictive, though the best writers by no means *limit* themselves to it, but use *which* as a restrictive frequently.

PROF. McKENZIE'S LECTURES.   167

THAT AND WHICH.

R = Restrictive ; C = Co-ordinate ; S = Superlative.

MACAULAY.

1. ... down to a time *which* is within the memory of men still living. | R
2. ... with a golden age *which* exists only in their imagination. | R
3. ... the task *which* I have undertaken ... | R
4. ... the revolutions *which* have taken place in dress ... | R
5. ... that contest *which* the administration of King James ... | R
6. ... the greatness *which* she was destined to attain ... | R
7. Of the western provinces *which* obeyed the Cæsars, she was the last THAT was conquered, and the first THAT was flung away. | R.S. (2)
8. The ... scanty civilization *which* the Britons had derived ... | R
9. The continental kingdoms *which* had risen... | R
10. The country *which* had been lost to view as Britain reappears as England. | R
11. Some things also *which* at a later period were justly regarded ... | R
12. ... who abhorred the pleasures ... *which* they had purchased by guilt ... | R
13. Many noble monuments *which* have since been destroyed ... | R
14. ... that great civilized world *which* had passed away. | R

168   PROF. McKENZIE'S LECTURES.

15. The same atrocities *which* had attended the victory... — R

16. ... founded a mighty state, *which* gradually extended its influence... — C

17. ... that dauntless valor *which* had been the terror... — R

18. ... the knowledge and refinement *which* they found in the country. — R

19. They raised their... language to a dignity ... *which* it had never before possessed. — R

20. That chivalrous spirit, *which* has exercised so powerful an influence... — R

21. ... every acquisition *which* they made... — R

22. ... an event *which* her historians have represented as disastrous... — R

23. ... England, *which*, since the battle of Hastings, had been ruled... by... — C

24. ... various tribes, *which* indeed all dwelt on English soil, but *which* regarded each other with aversion... — C(2)

25. ... those peculiarities *which* it has ever since retained... — R

26. ... that constitution *which* has... preserved its identity, and *which*... deserves to be regarded as the best... — R(2)

27. ... the archetype of all the representative assemblies *which* now meet... — R

28. Then it was that the colleges *which* still exist... were founded. — R

29. The war differed... from the wars *which* the Plantagenets had waged... — R

PROF. McKENZIE'S LECTURES. 169

30. ... the high and commanding qualities
which our forefathers displayed.   R
31. ... a superiority *which* was most striking
in the lowest ranks ...   R
32. ... and that the reverses *which* compelled
them to relinquish ...   R
33. ... the luxurious habits *which* prosperity
had engendered ...   R
34. ... the ... most salutary revolutions *which*
have taken place ... that revolution *which* ...
put an end to the tyranny ... and that revolu-
tion *which* put an end ...   R(2)
                    SCOTT.
35. ... beautiful hills ... *which* lie between
Sheffield and Doncaster.   R
36. ... the national convulsions *which* appeared
to be impending.   R
37. ... that independence *which* was so dear
to every English bosom ...   R
38. A circumstance *which* greatly tended to
enhance the tyranny ...   R
39. ... of that forest, *which* we have mentioned ..   R
40. ... wide-branched oaks, *which* had witness-
ed ... the march ...   C
41. ... the sun shot a broken ... light, THAT
partially hung upon the branches.   C
42. The human figures *which* completed this
landscape ...   R
43. ... of that wild and rustic character *which*
belonged ...   R
44. ... difficult to distinguish, from the patches
THAT remained ...   R

170   PROF. McKENZIE'S LECTURES.

45. ... two-edged knives ... *which* were fabri-
cated in the neighborhood ...   R
46. ... upon his head, *which* was only defend-
ed by his own ... hair ...   C
47. ... the overgrown beard ... *which* was rather of a yellow ...   C
48. ... a short cloak, *which* scarcely reached
half way down ...   C
49. ... those lingering hours, *which* they were
obliged to spend ...   R
50. ... dejection, *which* might be ... construed
into apathy ...   C
51. ... the fire *which* occasionally sparkled in
his ... eyes ...   R
52. ... The dialogue *which* they maintained ...
in Anglo-Saxon, *which* was universally spoken
by the inferior classes ...   C
53. ... the ... herd of swine, *which* ... made no
haste ...   C
54. ... a wolfish-looking dog ... *which* ran limp-
ing about ...   C
55. ... increased the evil *which* he seemed to
design to remedy ...   R
56. ... leave the herd to their destiny, *which* ...
can be little else ...   C
57. ... an opposite road from that *which* Wamba
had recommended ...   R
58. ... decline the task *which* they have aband-
oned.   R
59. ... through the outer stockade, *which* com-
municated by a drawbridge ...   C
60. ... a night like that *which* roars without ...   R

PROF. McKENZIE'S LECTURES   171

61. ...the fruit of all the glory *which* he had
acquired...   R
62. ...the same policy *which* had dictated the
conduct of their brethren...   R
63. ...the...meek good-nature *which* remained...merely the dregs of a character THAT
might have been deserving of praise...   R(2)
64. ...But on that *which* was to follow...   R
65. ...the place THAT once knew them, knows
them no more...   R
66. ...till we tell your Highness THAT which
we cannot know...   R
67. ...the good horse THAT was brought from
Barbary.   R
68. ...the noble armour THAT was worth so
many zecchins...   R
69. ...the full proportion of that *which* is her
due...   R
70. ...that honor *which* it became his privilege
to confer...   R

RUSKIN.

71. ...a perfection of any kind, *which* reason...
might have shown...   C
72. ...those large principles of right *which* are
applicable...   R
73. ...the only laws *which* resist it...are in-
applicable...   R
74. ...the new forms...of the art, *which* the
necessities...demand...   R
75. ...There is no law...*which* may not be
overthrown...   R
76. ...liable to errors *which* are avoided by the
present simplicity...   R

172   PROF. McKENZIE'S LECTURES.

77. ... mighty laws *which* govern the moral world ...   R
78. ... the ... value of the work, *which* is often small ...   C
79. The aspect of the years' THAT approach us is ... full of mystery ...   R
80. ... the exertion *which* every good man is called upon to put forth ...   R
81. ... the art *which* so disposes and adorns the edifices ...   R
82. ... extending principles *which* belong altogether|to building ...   R
83. ... all the various objections *which* may be urged against it ...   R
84. ... that *which* is especially concerned with the arts ...   R
85. ... the covenant THAT He made with men was accompanied ...   R
86. ... of the thought THAT invents, and the hand THAT labors ...   R
87. Of all THAT they have His tithe must be rendered to Him ...   R
88. ... there is not a building THAT I know of ...   R
89. ... one of the most frequent sources of pleasure *which* belongs to ... art ...   R
90. ... less the loss of labor THAT offends us, than the lack of judgment ...   R
91. ... adding ... enrichment to the deep shadows THAT relive the shafts ...   R

IRVING.

92. ... gray vapors about their summits, *which* ... glow and light up ...   C

PROF. McKENZIE'S LECTURES.   173

93. ...that meekness of spirit *which* gained
him...popularity...   R

94. ...his father's cast-off galligaskins, *which*
he had much ado to hold...   C

95. ...the only side *which*, in truth, belongs
to a henpecked husband.   R

96. ...a club of the sages...*which* held its
sessions on a bench...   R?

97. ...the profound discussions THAT sometimes took place...   R

98. ...on a green knoll...THAT crowned the
brow of the precipice...   R

99. ...a stout keg, THAT seemed full of
liquor...   C?

100. ...one of those transient thunder-showers
which often take place...   R

101. ...there was something strange...THAT
inspired awe...   C

102. ...nothing...but the noise of the balls,
which...echoed along...   C

103. He ventured...to taste the beverage,
which he found had...   C

104. ...entangled by the wild grape-vines
THAT twisted their coils...   R

105. ...rows of houses *which* he had never
seen before...   R

106. ...the great tree THAT used to shelter
the...inn...   R

107. ...and other words, *which* were a perfect
Babylonish jargon...   C?

108. ...a wooden tombstone... THAT used to
tell all about him...   R

174   PROF. McKENZIE'S LECTURES.

109. ...the strange events THAT had taken place...   R

EMERSON.

110. ...the originality *which* consists in weaving like the spider...   R

111. ...with the most determined aim *which* any man...knows...   R

112. ...he carries out the advice *which* her music gave him...   R

113. ...the tale of Troy, *which* the audience will bear hearing...   C

114. ...and other stories out of Plutarch, *which* they never tire of...   C

115. ...down to the royal Henries, *which* men hear eagerly...   C

116. ...the balance-wheel *which* the sculptor found in architecture...   R

117. ...materials...*which* had a certain excellence, *which* no...genius could create.   R

118. ...absorbs...all the light *which* is anywhere radiating...   R

119. ...all the debts *which* such a man could contract...   R

120. ...the very pieces *which* Shakespeare altered...   R

121. ...have...offered money for any information THAT will lead to proof...   R

122. ...under masks THAT are no masks to the intelligent...   R

123. ...think no criticism...valuable THAT does not rest on merit...,   R

PROF. McKENZIE'S LECTURES.   175

SALISBULY.

124. ... the kind language *which* our chairman
uttered ...   R
125. ... and discuss matters *which* attack our
feelings less deeply.   R
126. ... the great subjects *which* occupy the
minds of many ...   R
127. ... every important step *which* is taken by
my people.   R
128. ... a ... small section of opinion *which*
exists in this country.   R
129. ... condition of things *which* in critical
periods always occurs.   R
130. ... all the evils *which* we sincerely regret... R
131. You should sacrifice all THAT you have
done ...   R
132. ... a peace *which* will not last ...   R
133. It is the only thing *which* can make the
enterprise condemnable ...   R
134. ... a matter of business, *which* we must
push through ...   C ?
135. ... any restoration of peace *which* can
fully recognize ...   R
136. There is nothing THAT we so desire as a
peace *which* shall carry with it a fulfillment
of all our duties ...   R ?
137. ... an imposture *which* is not worth performing.   R
138. The impression *which* it will leave ...   R
139. ... any result THAT may commend itself...   R
140. ... this ... trying ... four years *which* we
have passed through ...   R

176   PROF. McKENZIE'S LECTURES.

141. ... responsibilities *which* do not at the moment appeal... R

142. ... questions of policy *which* will not pass away... R

ROSEBERY.

143. I feel an ignorance and humiliation *which* is almost abysmal... R

144. ... he ... remembers other fruits *which* have defeated his... R

145. ... haunted by the recollection of orchids *which* he does not possess.... R

146. ... enjoying all the variety *which* a garden can give. R

147. If he sees a weed *which* would distress an expert... R

148. ... We admire names *which* he sometimes remembers... R

149. There is nothing *which* pays so well as a book on gardening. R

150. ... the books THAT I love best on gardening... R

151. ... Lord Bacon's Essays, *which* contain one exquisite essay on gardening. C

152. ... sums up in a sentence the best THAT can be said... R.S.

153. ... who know everything THAT is to be known... R

154. ... The passage ... *which* will illustrate what I mean... C

155. Another kind of book THAT you might read... R

156. ... countries *which* are redolent of the history which you have read... R(?)

PROF. McKENZIE'S LECTURES. 177

157. That is a little recipe of my own *which* I give to you... R

158. ...the noble statue *which* I am about to unveil... R

159. ...marvelled at the secular reverence *which* enbalms his memory... R

160. ...romantic elements *which* fascinate successive generations... R

161. ...the highest qualities *which* we cherish.. R

162. That was a quality *which* was then rare among princes... R

163. He did for them all THAT, in their barbarous condition, they required. R

164. ...the founder of the London *which* we know... R

165. ...the awful destinies *which* awaited him... R

166. ...the England *which* was to be... R

167. ...that jurisprudence *which* he himself had raised from the dead... R

168. ...the...nations *which* own the..fatherhood of the British crown. R

169. ...the origin of much THAT makes England powerful. R

170. ...that...development *which* has glorified the life of our cities... R

171. It is the one *which* is given without undue influence. R

BALFOUR.

172. ...the difficulty of the task *which* the government have undertaken... R

173. ...the difficult controversies *which* any attempt must involve... R

178   PROF. McKENZIE'S LECTURES.

174. ... the great problem *which*, for ... years
past, education has presented ...   R
175. There was nothing ... *which* could properly be described as a ... system ...   R
176. ... filling up gaps ... *which* the existing
system then suffered from ...   R
177. ... the vacuum *which* voluntary effort did
not succeed in filling up ...   R
178. ... a competition *which* was certainly not
anticipated ...   R
179. The act of 1889, *which* gave to county
councils duties ...   C
180. It is not the system *which* would be
tolerated ...   R
181. ... the magnitude of the cost *which* the
two ... services throw on us ...   R

                    MORLEY.

182. ... the rising of the tide to the ... height
which would float him ...   R
183. I will take a case *which* ought to interest
you citizens.   R
184. ... the budget of 1853, *which* revealed to
the country ...   C
185. ... with that 'force *which* was too powerful for any mind to resist ...   R
186. This revolution *which* he effected ...   R
187. ... like a shelving beach *which* restrained
the waves ...   R
188. He made an opinion *which* ... guided the
policy of the country ...   R
189. He misread the civil war in America
which saved the ... Union ...   C

PROF. McKENZIE'S LECTURES. 179

190. Here is a passage *which* I always like
to read myself.   R
CLEVELAND.

191. ... bonds of the United States *which* were
therin ... specified ...   R

192. ... there remained of the gold *which* had
been provided ...   R

193. This is the fund *which* has since them
been called ...   R

194. ... gold certificates, *which* ... resemble a
bank's certificate ...   C

195. ... a law was passed by Congress *which*
provided ...   R

196. ... another law of Congress *which* had
much to do with ... the financial conditions
THAT necessitated the issue of ... bonds.   R

197. ... in excess of the sum THAT had come
to be ... regarded ...   R

198. ... the distrust, *which* was growing enor-
mously, regarding the wisdom ...   R

199. ... the prospect THAT greeted the new
administration ...   R

200. ... no bid would be considered THAT did
not offer a premium ...   R

201. ... the only government bonds *which* could
be sold ...   R

202. ... a time ... of depression greater than
any THAT had ... darkened ...   R

203. ... the real trouble *which* confronts us
consists in a lack ...   R

204. The ... events ... suggest ... facts *which*
should .. arrest attention.   R

180   PROF. McKENZIE'S LECTURES.

205. ... leave nothing undone *which* furnishes
a hope for improving...   R
206. ... the terms THAT would give the appearance of impaired... credit.   R
207. ... the amount *which* would be saved to
the Government...   R
208. ... a response THAT would accord with
patriotic public duty...   R
209. ... the "endless chain" *which* had...
drained our gold...   R
2I0. Another difficulty THAT had to some extent prevented...   R

MILTON.

211. ... no other than the joy ... *which* it brings
to all...   R
212. ... by the very sound of this *which* I shall
utter...   R
213. ... if one of your orders, *which* I should
name, were called...   C
214. ... than other courts, *which* had produced
nothing worth memory...   C?
215. ... the form of democracy *which* was then
established.   R
216. ... that love of the truth *which* ye...
profess...   R
217. ... that uprightness of judgment *which*
is not... partial...   R
218. ... by judging... that order *which* ye have
ordained...   R
219. ... libellous books, *which* were... intended
to be suppressed...   C

PROF. McKENZIE'S LECTURES.   181

220. ...by hindering...the discovery THAT
might be yet further made...   R

221. ...only two sorts of writings *which* the
magistrate cared...   R

222. ...they met with no interdict THAT can
be cited...   R

223. ...the book... *which* they so dealt with...   R

224. ...a violation worse than any (that) could
be offered...   (R)

225. ...licensing of that *which* they say Clau-
dius intended...   R

226. ...the most tyrannous Inquisition THAT
ever inquired...   R.S.

227. ...for the tree THAT bore it...   R

228. ...and whether be more the benefit or the
harm THAT thence proceeds...   R

229. ...with great odds on that side *which*
affirmed it...   R

230. ...bred by the fever *which* had then
seized him...   R

231. ...grow...upon those things *which* hereto-
fore were governed...   R

232. ...burnt those books *which* were their
own...   R

233. That virtue, therefore, *which* is but a
youngling, and knows not the utmost THAT
vice promises to her followers...   R(2)

234. ...all the contagion THAT foreign books
can infuse...   R.S.

235. ...It was the task *which* I began with...   R

236. ...the epigrams and dialogues *which* he
made...   R

182   PROE. McKENZIE'S LECTURES.

237. ...the severest discipline THAT can be
exercised...   R. S.
              ADDISON.
238. ...a gray pad THAT is kept in the
stable...   R
239. ...the joy THAT appeared in the coun-
tenances of ... domestics...   R
240. ...tinged by a certain extravagance, *which*
makes them particularly his...   C
241. ...all the good sermons *which* have been
printed in English...   R
242. ...all those other talents THAT are
proper...   R
243. ...the returns of affection... *which* are
paid him by every one THAT lives within his
neighborhood.   R
244. ...that general respect *which* is shown to
the good old knight.   R
245. ...that great appearance and solemnity
which... accompaines...   R
246. ...the alterations THAT he had ordered
to be made in it.   R
247. ...the summit of a rock THAT was not
far from me...   R
248. ...those heavenly airs THAT are played
to the departed souls...   R
249. ...trap-doors that lay concealed... *which*
the passengers... trod upon...   R.C.
250. ...thrusting several persons on trap-doors,
which did not seems to lie in their way...   C ?

PROFESSOR ELLIOTT'S LECTURES.

CHAPTER I.

INTRODUCTORY TO ORAL READING.

Prof. Elliott, a Canadian gentleman of amiable manners, with face cleanly shaved, came on the platform and spoke as follows:—

"This being my first experience in being called upon to deliver lectures at a Teachers' Summer School, I was somewhat at a loss as to what topic to choose. After much consideration, I took up "Reading" as my principal subject, as I thought it would be a very suitable one in your case. Good readers are by no means plenty even in the lands where English is spoken,—whether it be in my native land—Canada—in England, or in America. It is not to be wondered at, therefore, that you (Japanese), to whom English is an adopted language, find a great deal of difficulty in this particular branch of language study. I thought over the question of choosing a book of reference, to illustrate my theory. Kanda's series of 'Readers' is admirably well compiled, and might have been chosen with advantage; but, since I have not personally taught with them, I thought I had better make use of 'Esop's Fables,' which I use at the Hiroshima Higher Normal School."

He then began his lecture by saying that the first principle to be observed in reading is to be *natural*. "You have" he said, „a forma lstyle of reading,

184 PROF. ELLIOTT'S LECTURES.

peculiar to the Japanese people, and you do not attempt to read as you speak. Not so with English. We are required indeed to read various kinds of style, —colloquial, descriptive, argumentative, literary,—but, in every case, the reading should be as natural, that is, conversational, as possible. Yet the advice: 'Read naturally' is not safe or sufficient even at home. In Japan it is of no use whatever. We who speak English as our native language read colloquial sentences with more ease and perfection than other styles, whereas Japanese students of English generally find them harder than the others. You do well to practice reading of this kind; for a great deal in common English books is written in this style, and, besides, it is of much practical use to you as affording much help in conversation. In reading, you should ever be careful to digest the underlying thought, and find what words in a passage are of the greatest importance. You should also endeavor to attain to good reading by imitating good speaking, and trying to be first of all good conversationalists. The best reader is an actor: his reading makes a strong impression upon his hearers, because he makes it real and life-like, by placing himself exactly under the conditions which it portrays. This was illustrated by an incident connected with the reading of a passage in which occurred the words, "the smelling of newmown hay."

The professor then put what he intended to lecture about into four heads,—Pause, Inflection, Pronunciation and Emphasis. Pronunciation, he told us, he would treat briefly, making only some general statements, as Prof. Gauntlett was to dwell on it at length.

PROF. ELLIOTT'S LECTURES. 185

1. Pause.

Pause, loosely, is a rest or stopping of voice according to the punctuation marks used. The pause is shortest at the comma ; longer at the semicolon, colon, dash, and exclamation and interrogation marks when they are not used at the end of a sentence ; longest at a period or other marks at the end of a sentence. But pause and the use of these punctuation marks do not necessarily correspond. There is a pause, independent of these punctuation marks, which is called the Rhetorical Pause. There are many instances of Rhetorical Pause where there is no break in the sense, and so no mark used. This generally happens when two emphatic words come in succession, not closely related together in thought, as : "Pleasure bought with *pains hurts*" (meaning, Pleasure hurts when bought with pains.) Here the pause comes between the two last words, the stronger emphasis being on the last. "He will stay here ; *she there.*" In this sentence the pause comes between *she* and *there*, and the latter word is the more emphatic.

The conjunction that, introducing a noun clause, but followed immediately by a modifying expression, must be followed by a comma ; and a Nominative of Address, immediately following something spoken to the person addressed, be preceded by a comma ; but in both cases, the comma has very little value in reading—i. e., there is very little pause.

Example 1.

"I think that, in such a case, I had better *stay.*"

In this sentence, the strongest emphasis is on the last word ; but, besides, there being emphasis on *think,*

186   PROF. ELLIOTT'S LECTURES.

and not on *that* (which is now treated as a conjunction, though in old English it was regarded as a demonstrative pronoun) there must be a pause between these two; while, on the other hand, though there is a comma after *that*, the pause there is very slight.

Example 2.

"Come here, John."

There is a comma between *here* and *John*, but scarcely any pause. The last word is non-emphatic.

Example 3.

"John, come here."

In this sentence, there is a pause between *John* and *come*, because the nominative of address (*John*) precedes. In this case, John is somewhat emphatic.

Some writers, then, are inaccurate in defining punctuation marks as indicating pause of voice rather than break of thought. They also err in making the colon only mark a longer pause of voice than a semicolon : a colon has a distinct *pointing* function (pointing forward), as: "Virtue is better than vice : it leaves a man with a clearer conscience ; it secures for him the confidence of others," etc. This quotation also illustrates another rule for the use of the colon : When several clauses, separated by semicolons, follow a general statement to fill out or explain its meaning, they are separated from it by a colon.

This function of pointing forward is also seen in its kindred uses : *Dear Sir:* (at the beginning of a letter) ; Marquis Ito said : (preceding a formal address or quotation, a proverb, etc.).

In a parenthesis, whether more distinctly marked

PROF. ELLIOTT'S LECTURES. 187

(by dashes or brackets) or less distinctly (by commas), the ordinary force is given to the principal clause (containing the parenthesis), while the part in the parenthesis is read quickly and lightly; as:

1. "A Wolf, *having a bone stuck in his throat,* * hired a Crane, *for a large sum,* * to put her head into her throat, and draw out the bone."

2. "One of them, *an exceedingly old one* * (*for many a field had he ploughed*), thus spoke:..."

Reference was again made to the use of the colon, that it has demonstrative force, and is also used to introduce a formal or long quotation, while the comma precedes a short or informal one.

He then advised us to be deliberate in reading; not to read in a hurry, but rather pause frequently at first,—that is, by dividing the sentences into reading phrases. It is well to read slow and sure, rather than quickly and unintelligibly. He had scarcely proceeded to the subject of Inflection when the bell rang, announcing the stop of the lecture. Wherefore he promised to begin this subject again on the following day, and left the platform.

---

* These parts are very slightly parenthetical.

CHAPTER II.

ORAL READING.

Previous to entering upon the subject of Inflection, the lecturer briefly repeated the essential part of his lecture of the preceding day, emphasizing particularly the fact that the fundamental idea of Reading is that of being natural ; that is to say, to speak in an expressive, conversational way the thought contained in the sentences.

He then came to the subject of Inflection, and said that the word literally means *bending*, and is a peculiar cadence used to express varying shades of thought and feeling. There are three inflections :

1. The Rising Inflection, a tone curving upward. Used only in interrogations, in expressing surprise or doubt, as :

1. " Should I ? "

2. " Is that ass your own ? One would not think so by the way you load him " (conveying the idea of doubt or surprise).

3. " Are you, with such a mind, going to be a king over beasts ? " (conveying the idea of surprise or contempt).

4. Indeed ? (surprise)

5. " Is he here ? " (surprise)

6. " Is he out ? " (surprise)

PROF. ELLIOTT'S LECTURES.   189

7. "Did you say no?"

The rising inflection is not used so often as Japanese students seem to think; only when a sentence conveys some such idea as surprise, or doubt, or censure.

2. The Falling Inflection,—a tone curving downward. It is by far the most commonly used inflection—on every emphatic word where neither the rising nor circumflex is used; on the last words of all sentences that end in periods:—on the last words of the longer independent clauses of compound sentences; and on the last word of the principal statement of any sentence or long independent clause, even when it is followed by some qualifying expression, provided that expression is long or distinct enough to cause a break in the sense between it and the principal statement. As an illustration of the last case, take the following sentence: "He came back soon, to the great joy of his friends." Here the falling inflection must be given at "soon," as well as at the end of the sentence. It is marked thus: ⟍ , in contrast to the mark, ⟋ , used in the case of a rising inflection.

Example:

"I don't live in a town; I live in a city."

3. The Circumflex,—a rising and a falling inflection comblined. It is sometimes a slight rising and a prolonged falling—the falling circumflex ; and some times a slight falling and a prolonged rising—the rising circumflex. The circumflex is marked thus: ∧. It is generally used on the last word of conditional (sign: *if*) or concessive (sign : *though, although*) clauses, or of a clause immediately before one containing an ad-

190 PROF. ELLIOTT'S LECTURES.

versative (contrasting) conjunction (sign: *but, however*), when such word is emphatic, as:

1. "Your feathers are all very well in the spring, but mine protect me in the winter" (the last word before an adversative conjunction).

2. "If he comes, I will go (conditional); though I die, I will go" (concessive).

3. "My son, I am afraid that you are not only blind, but that you have lost your sense of smell."

At times the condition, concession, contrast, etc. is only implied and not formally expressed, as:

1. "If your owner had found thee, and not I" (= If not I, but your owner...).

2. "The value is in the worth, not in the number" (=not in the number, but.....—contrast implied).

3. But when the birds found that the sling was only swung in the air, ... (=though swung in the air, it......—concessive idea implied).

The circumflex is also used to express sarcasm or reproach, as:

1. "You are a fine fellow" (sarcasm—rising circum).

2. "He connot eat the hay himself, and yet refuses to allow those who to eat who can" (reproach).

The lecturer then alluded to the subject of Pronunciation briefly, for Mr. Gauntlett was, as he

PROF. ELLIOTT'S LECTURES.

said, going to deal with it very minutely. He simply said that pronunciation can be mastered only by careful attention to the best speakers and dictionaries, and by constant practice. To the Japanese student it is at once very difficult and very important to acquire a good pronunciation, because of the few opportunities he has of listening to good speakers of English. Many excellent English scholars among the Japanese pronounce badly, and he ascribed the reason to want of practice, under the direction of good speakers. If schools can afford to be taught by two foreign teachers of English, it would be advisable to employ one Englishman and one American ; for it is well for students to learn the pronunciation of both. Some speak English without many mistakes, but their pronunciation is bad ; others make many blunders in speaking but their pronunciation is good. The latter is preferable, in his opinion, to the former. If a style of pronunciation becomes fixed, it can not be easily corrected ; but imperfect syntax can be corrected at any stage. Care must be taken, therefore, in teaching beginners in particular.

As authoritative English dictionaries, he recommended the "Century," "Standard," "Oxford," and "Imperial."

CHAPTER III.

ORAL READING.

Mr. Elliott wrote on the board a quotation he used the day before yesterday, and said that someone had asked him to explain it. The quotation is as follows: "Pleasure bought with *pains hurts.*" He gave a full explanation in plain English, so I have no doubt that the intelligent questioner was quite satisfied with it· The professor then mentioned a few important points in relation to Inflection which he omitted on the preceding day. He explained again that the *Rising Inflection* (a curving of the voice upwards) is used only in questions which express surprise or doubt. In double questions, the rising inflection does not come twice in succession, as :

"Is he here, or there?"
"No" represents several meanings according to inflection. For instance, in answer to the question, "Will he be here next week?" suppose we say "No," then the meaning is that it is not his intention now, but if you would like him to stay, or if it suits you, he may stay. Then when we say "No" (ordinary falling inflection) to such a question as, "Will he go home this week?" it simply denotes an ordinary negative. Again when we say "No" to such a question as "Won't he really?" then it shows an emphatic

PROF. ELLIOTT'S LECTURES.   193

negative. The circumflex sign, " ∧," is often used
in a case like this.

Next came a few suggestions on the subject of Pronunciation, in addition to those of the previous lecture
To acquire the right accent is a difficult task even for
Englishmen and Americans. Japanese students need
special drill on accent and on all short vowel sounds.
They do not put sufficient force on the accented syllable, so in teaching it, it may be well to exaggerate
somewhat at first. Some short vowel and consonant
sounds in which they should be practised are *ŏ* and
â; *b, v, f*; *s* and *sh*; *ōō* and *woo*; *n* and *ng*; *th* and
th. The unaccented syllables are sometimes too much
drawn out, and the vowel sound of these given too
much value or force, particularly in words ending in
ănt, ănce, ăncy, āte, ātely. For instance, such words
as dist*ant*, const*ancy*, affection*ate*, commensur*ate* have
mute vowel sounds in the last syllables, and should
be pronounced by Japanese students as if there were
no vowel or vowel sound at all.

He then proceeded to the subject of Emphasis.
Emphasis is one of the most important features in
reading, and denotes a stress of voice on a word, but
sometimes on a syllable, as: (a) "*He*, not she, is
coming." (b) "To *in*crease and *de*crease..." In
ordinary use, the accent is on the second syllable in
each of these verbs, but in case contrast is implied,
—or they are in antithesis,—the stress comes on the
first syllables. *Grateful* and *un*grateful is another
example of this kind. "*Un*," "*in*" and "*de*" are in
reality word-forms, and often emphasized when the
words containing them are in antithesis. This may

194   PROF. ELLIOTT'S LECTURES.

simply be called a change of accent, but the professor considers it a case of emphasis. In general, words performing the *more* important functions are more emphatic : nouns, verbs, and interjections, rather than prepositions, conjunctions, pronouns, and articles. The emphatic and non-emphatic use of adjectives and adverbs is about equal : this is determined by the construction of particular sentences. Articles, pronouns, conjunctions, and prepositions are of minor importance so far as meaning is concerned, and are only emphasized for some special reason. As an example showing the more frequently emphasized parts of speech in an ordinary sentence, the following was given :

"*Wonderful!* I *looked* and *saw* him at the *side* of the *road.*

CHAPTER IV.

ORAL READING.

The lecturer first expressed his idea with regard to a question found in the "Question Box," as to how to read poems. He asserted that there was no special manner of reading poems, no material difference between poem-reading and prose-reading. Let it suffice to say that the principal aim in each is to give expression naturally to the underlying thought involved in the passage. It is a common mistake to pause at the end of every line of poetry, or to stop at the end of every foot. We call that *scanning;* that is to say, a mechanical reading which is not really reading at all.

Then he continued his lecture on Emphasis. The last part of what he mentioned was that pronouns, articles, prepositions, and conjunctions are unemphatic in most cases. But any word, even articles, may become emphatic for some special reason. The great question which one must answer in order to place the emphasis properly is, "What is the chief thought intended in the expression?" For instance, in the following sentences, "Why do you steal?" "Because father is dead, and it is as much as I can do to get bread," "steal," "dead," and "to get bread" are emphatic, because they express the principal ideas in the sentences.

The most important principle (or special reason) affecting a change in the ordinary emphasis is An-

PROF. ELLIOTT'S LECTURES.

tithesis (or Contrast), which sets one idea or thought over against another. This may change the emphasis in two ways :

1. By putting the emphasis on words not emphatic without some special reason, as :
" *I* (= not you) went." " I went *and* saw (= both went and saw) him."

2. By putting extra emphasis on words already emphatic, as : " I **went** (I did not stand and look) and saw him at the **side** (not in middle) of a river."

The second term of an antithesis is the stronger, as : " *went*, but soon **returned**." This is *sweet ;* you said it was **sour**."

CHAPTER V.

ORAL READING.

The subject of Emphasis was continued. When double or multiple antitheses come together, they follow usually the order of importance, the more important having the stronger emphasis, as : (1) " This is *sweet; that* **sour** " (double antitheses). (2) " *Your feathers* are all very well in the **spring**, but **mine** protect me against the WINTER " (double antitheses). (3) If you had as many *brains* in your **head** as you heve **hairs** in your BEARD, you would never have gone DOWN before you had inspected the way **UP** " (triple antitheses—3 pairs). If the order of words change, though they express the same thought, yet the relative emphasis changes, as :

" In *spring* it is all very well to have **your feathers,** but in **win**.**er** to be protected by MINE."

Antitheses are not always so regular, or their terms so near each other, as :

1. " I would rather have *one* **barleycorn** than ALL the **jewels** IN THE WORLD." (ALL and IN THE WORLD are separated, but they are to be united in thought, as conjointly modifying " jewels.")

2. " As they were disputing, they passed a statue, carved in stone, which represented " a Lion strangled by a man." The traveller pointed to it and said : " See there ! How strong we are, and how we prevail

198   PROF. ELLIOTT'S LECTURES.

over even the king of beasts." The Lion replied :
"That statue was made by one of your men. If we
Lions knew how to erect statues, you would see the
Man placed under the paw of the Lion." Here 1, 2 ;
3, 4 ; and 5,6 constitute three pairs of antitheses, of
the terms of which 1 is the least, and 4 the most,
emphatic.

3. " ' Everything is ready but you ; so come with
me instantly.' The Dog wagging his tail, replied :
' Oh, master ! I am quite ready ; it is you for whom
I am waiting.' " Here 1,2 constitute an antithesis ;
then 2, again, with 5 constitute a second ; then,
finally,, 3 (or 4, which is simply a repetition of 3)
and 5 constitute a third, Hence 1 is the weakest
term, and 5 the strongest. But it should be noted
that while the stress is laid on 2 by speaking in a
loud voice, it is laid on 3 rather by dwelling long
on the word, because 2 is in an expression of angry
reproach, while 3 is in one of meek but decided
expostulation.

In a series of clauses where the same expression
recurs in each that expression is emphatic in only
one, usually the 1st, as : "I asked his *name ;* he *told*
me his name." "The rustic driver did nothing but
utter loud cries to *Hercules.* Hercules, it is said,
appeared." The words conveying the chief ideas of
a clause, are the most important, and the same words
are unlikely to be repeated as most important in
successive clauses.

PROF. ELLIOTT'S LECTURES.   199

In a climax the last term is the most emphatic, the others grading up to it. All enumerations or series of terms of the same order are treated somewhat like climaxes, and the strongest emphasis is placed on the last term, as : " *Book* and **table** ; " " *Book*, **box**, and TABLE." " The Frogs, grieved at having no established Ruler, *sent ambassadors* to Jupiter asking for *a* King. He cast a huge log into the lake. They thought themselves ill-treated in the appointment of so inert a ruler, and sent a **2nd deputation** to pray for **another** sovereign. He gave them an Eel. The Frogs thought him *too good-natured, and a* THIRD TIME sent to him to beg for ANOTHER King. Jupiter, displeased, sent a Heron, who soon left none to croak on the lake." Here 1,2,3 make up one series of the same order, and 4,5,6 another. In 2 and 3 it is the use of the terms " 2nd " and " 3rd " which really make them a part of a series, and the 1st member of the series—the expression *1st*—does not appear at all, but is implied in 1, considered in relation to 2 & 3. This Fable of " The Frogs Asking for a King," especially when not abbreviated as above, illustrates also the fact that sometimes the terms of a series are considerably separated from each other, and that some care is needed to remember their proper order and relations. But experience makes this easy.

The nominative of address is not emphatic when it follows what is addressed to the person spoken to, or any part of it, as : " **Help** *me*, father." (The com-

200   PROF. ELLIOTT'S LECTURES.

ma has no special force, but is only intended for in-
telligibility.) Sometimes, when the nominative of
address is modified by strong epithets, it is emphatic,
as : " *You foolish old fellow!* " (implying censure or
ridicule). In compound verbal forms, abstract nouns
prepositions, adverbs complements, direct objects, or
infinitives (the last three not strictly constituents of
compounds, but may be treated in the same way for
reading purposes) are more emphatic than the verbal
forms to which they are joined, as : " Make *haste* ; "
" go *away* ; " to drive *nails* ; " it is *white* ; " " came
to *see* ; " " bring it *up*." This is because these added
words give to the verbal forms their distinctive character or meaning in the expressions in which they are
used. (The last phrase may be grammatically written
" bring up it," but " it " is made to precede " up " for
the sake ef euphony.)

When two words, both emphatic, come together,
but are not closely related in thought, the second is
generally more emphatic than the first, as : " *Pleasure*
brought with **pains** HURTS."

CHAPTER VI.

METHOD IN THE STUDY OF ENGLISH.

This morning Mr. Elliott said it was his intention to devote this hour and the next two or three first hours of each day to a discussion of method in the study of English. The question of "method" seems to be emphasized more than is necessary in Japan. Good teachers are needed always even more than good methods—those who are thoroughly versed in their subjects, enthusiastic and conscientious in their work, and who are ready to adopt any method, provided it will make their instruction effective as well as interesting. No teacher should be a slave to any particular method. He should indeed have the advantage of normal training ; but the good teacher will learn much from his own experience, will have certain fundamental principles of his own, and will shape largely his own methods.

In America normal training is now so much appreciated that, besides numberless public schools, there are a good many Sunday schools where normal-trained teachers are employed. That is, normal training is found most useful not only in secular teaching but also in religious teaching. By such means teachers get valuable suggestions and help which make them much more qualified for their work than they used to be.

But, in reality, a true teacher, like a poet, is " born,

202   PROF. ELLIOTT'S LECTURES.

"not made." He is endowed with, certain teaching instincts, especially that of adoptability. He does not undertake to explain much, but makes his students think; he does not always correct mistakes directly, but puts his students on the track of discovering their blunders themselves. He studies and understands the individuality of his pupils, and teachers accordingly. He is well aware how far his class is advanced in knowledge, and if he finds anyone below the level, he makes him reach it. He encourages the shy and the nervous, by addressing them in easy and simple language, and causes them to be more like themselves. Again, when he finds those who try to show how much they know, or to discover weak points in a teacher—and there are such young fellows—he puts on them a little restraint, by means of a few well-directed questions, or some other good means, until they understand their limitations and are sufficiently repressed. Here the professor alluded to a student of his school, who had the bad habit of putting on knowing airs. When the student first came to Hiroshima, he spoke to him with a great show of his linguistic knowledge, and said very fluently, "Oh, Mr. Elliott, I am very glad to see you firstly," and so on. In the class, he always watched for a chance to show himself off. The professors of the school adopted the repressive method, and did much to break him of his offensive habit; and he has developed into one of the best students in the school.

"But," remarked Mr. Elliott, "though good teachers is the most essential thing, still the question of method is not to be slighted." Method, though of

PROF. ELLIOTT'S LECTURES.   203

subordinate importance, is certainly important. There
are certainly crude, and even bad, methods. Many
teachers tell rather than suggest. Now, in teaching
foreign languages, the two important points which
claim our attention are: 1. Suggestion (not direct
explanation or teaching). 2. General principles first,
and special rules afterwards. Lay down the general
first, and build upon this foundation the more particular. Besides, we are required to be accurate in
our work; in other words, the principle of thorough-
ness in the work must he insisted upon; otherwise,
we fail to make the students really and quickly advance by our instruction.

There is no one method which is perfect by itself.
The best method is invariably a combination of a variety of approved methods. Some make it their method
to give their chief attention to conversation books in
language study; some to grammar; still others to
the listening intently to the best speakers. These
methods are effective in case they go together, but
when taken separately, anyone of them is found in-
sufficient. Hence the best form of the question is:
" What are the best methods?" not " What is the best
method?"

Mr. Elliott spoke now particularly about the best
methods in the study of English Reading. There was
one kind of reading which was relatively simple, and
in connection with it the question of the best methods
must be decided upon by Japanese teachers, rather
than by foreign teachers; so the professor would not
deal with it. This was the private reading of the
man who was only seeking information, and where

204 PROF. ELLIOTT'S LECTURES.

the chief need was simply to understand the author's meaning.

He then called the attention of the audience to some methods in the study of "Oral Reading" "You need to be thoroughly acquainted with it," he said, "almost a specialist in it, if you hope to climb to the summit of the Fujisan of English conversation."

It is always advisable, in the lower classes at least, and in some higher ones, that the teachers of translation should go over the reading lessons first, and see that the meaning is well understood, before they are taken up for oral reading. The instructor who is capable of teaching oral reading, whether a foreigner or not, is more expensive to the school than a teacher of translation, and it is better to use him to the best advantage, by keeping him at work along this special line, and not take too much of his time in unravelling the meaning. It is very important for a teacher to require his pupils to practise their reading before coming to the class, especially those who through nervousness are apt to read fast. Call the attention of your class to punctuation, the careful study of which has much to do with good reading. A teacher should be practical and at the same time careful in his teaching, and should not allow any mistakes or blunders to escape his eyes or ears.

He then called attention again to the relation between conversation and oral reading—which he had spoken of in previous lectures—and reminded us that, in the case of beginners, a teacher had better read and have them follow him all together, and then make one of them read, correcting his mistakes as he pro-

PROF. ELLIOTT'S LECTURES.

ceeds. By this means, they will not have quite so much individual practice, but every member will have more frequent practice. In a more advanced class, let a student read first, in his turn, and others criticize him, the teacher giving a model reading after, and having the student read again. By this latter method the students will go over only a little ground in a given time, but they improve much. Sentences should be broken into words or phrases, in the case of beginners, so as to have them avoid pausing where it can not be permitted, or reading too much at one breath. Example:

"I went | and asked him | to surrender | —unconditionally | to surrender." These are called "reading phrases" in contrast to "grammatical phrases." If a pause is made at the wrong place, the ear of the trained teacher will detect it at once, even when he is not looking at the book.

CHAPTER VII.

METHOD IN THE STUDY OF ENGLISH.

Mr. Elliott briefly referred to what he lectured on the day before. Students should thoroughly understand the lessons before they attempt to read them. And they should not handle difficult books until they are well-trained in simpler ones—should not take up the Fifth Reader when their English knowledge is fitted only to study the First or Second. The main point which we should always keep in view in reading is to acquaint ourselves with idiomatic phrases, the construction of sentences, the style peculiar to English. For this purpose the easier "Readers" are better than advanced books, which contain difficult literary phraseology.

In dictation, as in reading, class criticism may be adopted with much advantage. Among the various methods for the teaching of dictation, he thinks one of the best is to send, say, four boys to the blackboard; let the first write one passage, another a different one, and so on, until all have written. Meanwhile all keep their books closed. The teacher then reads the text as it is, and makes the other boys criticize the passages written on the board. By means of this method students help one another, and decided interest is created.

He then proceeded to the topic of conversation. The two important principles that should be observed in conversation, are:

PROF. ELLIOTT'S LECTURES.

1. Imitation.
2. Memorising.

By imitation is meant the endeavor to master pronunciation, intonation, accentuation, etc. by following the best speakers, and trying to make every sound exactly as they do. Without the faculty of imitation one can never be natural in speaking a foreign tongue. There are some Japanese whose tone and accent are so much like those of an Englishman or American that when heard out of sight they are taken for these. This is the highest achievement in conversation; but it cannot be attained without being bold and free in imitation.

Memorising must include committing to memory various idomatic phrases and the colloquial expressions in daily use. It is not enough to memorise merely words, for they are of little avail in conversation unless we can readily bring them into their common order and relations to each other. Like bricks, their use lies in their proper building and combination. It is, therefore, always advisable for students to memorize the phraseology that is in habitual use. And such idioms and colloquial phrases should be constantly made use of, when occasion arises. By such practice and application the students will one day find themselves able to speak without any great effort.

There are some who are weak in memory, but have excellent ability in imitation ; while others have a good retentative memory, though their power of imitation is defective. Nevertheless, in either case, a good teacher can make them good speakers by drilling them specially on their weaker side. But when one is found deficient in both of these faculties, then

208   PROF. ELLIOTT'S LECTURES.

teaching becomes difficult indeed: in that case, a
teacher can only do his best to push the pupil on
slowly and steadily. Memorizing is hard work, but
it cannot be helped: the attaining of proficiency in
conversation is admittedly laborious and dishearten-
ing; one needs dogged perseverance. Only thus can
one succeed.

"Should books be used in conversation?" he said.
"Yes, I am firmly convinced that books can be used
with advantage in it—books in which a large assort-
ment of common phrases and expressions all ready
for immediate use are found in good order. But they
must be good—there must be no doubt whatever as
to the quality of the English. Never use any conversation book that has not been revised by an educated
man whose native tongue is English. Those written
by experienced and successful Japanese teachers of
English, in conjunction with foreigners of the same
class, are preferable; for they, are useful for both
Japanese students and for English-speaking people
studying the Japanese tongue."

He then mentioned a few books which are particularly useful in the practical study of English.
They are as follows:

"Scenes from English Life," by Swan and Bètis;

"English Etymology," by Imbrie;

"Natural Lessons," by McKenzie;

The Conversation Exercises in Kanda's series of
Readers;

Saito's Conversation-Grammar books.

Among the books above referred to, the professor
recommended "Naturals Lessons" and English Ety-

PROF. ELLIOTT'S LECTURES. 209

mology" in particular. In reference to the latter, he said that he had looked into or used a considerable number of conversation books, but he had always come back to Imbrie's Etymology, though it was first published more than fifteen years ago. The work is somewhat large, owing to considerable theory, useful mainly to foreigners, and so is somewhat dear; but the exercises are in the best colloquial English.

Not only are good books needed, but a wise judgment in the use of them. Much care must be taken in distinguishing synonyms and variations, and making clear what really are synonyms and variations and what are not. Take, for example, such words as "change," "alter;" "mend," "repair;" "correct." In such a sentence as "I must get my fence mended," "corrected" could not be used at all, and "altered" would convey quite a different meaning. It is one of the chief duties of the teacher to clear up the confused ideas students have of synonyms. The same is true of variations. It is also very necessary that he should make sure that they know exactly what the exercises, as memorized, mean, and, specially, what they mean when slightly changed by him in form, by a variation of voice, mood, tense, or some other. And so, in many ways, the proper *use* of books, important in any branch of language-study, is especially so in conversation. That education means "*drawing out*"—drawing out what mental powers and gifts students naturally have, and not packing disorderly pieces of knowledge into their heads—is something which must be remembered by the teacher

210   PROF. ELLIOTT'S LECTURES.

always. Not simply to allow students to follow mechanically or blindly the lines and suggestions only of anyone else, however wise he may be, but to be always a directing force, a creator of variety and enthusiasm, an exploiter of the latent talent of the student, so that he may become truly hearty and intelligent in his work—that is the ideal. The teacher must always take part, even when, as may often be profitably done, he has the students converse with one another.

CHAPTER VIII.

METHOD IN THE STUDY OF ENGLISH.

Mr. Elliott continued his lecture on the method of giving lessons in English conversation. The general outline of his lecture is as follows :

Some people do not approve of free conversation in the class room. But he could not see why students should not speak freely in English, if the teacher is careful to correct every error as it occurs. This he should do, even at the expense of their little prepared talks, which are sometimes better upset and broken up, being stiff, grandiose and otherwise unnatural. There is need to show the student that conversation is not necessarily, or even chiefly, a matter of asking and answering questions. Another need is to show him the importance of using simple expressions. But above all it is necessary to teach him accuracy. Do not pass over any mistake, unless very trivial indeed. By accuracy he did not mean " *Chokuyaku,*" which must be ruled out whenever it conflicts with natural, idiomatic English. To translate Japanese literally does not moke true English. For instance, if we were to literally translate the Japanese phrase, " *Ame ga futte mo yari ga futte mo,*" as " Even though it should rain, or spears should fall," it would be very unusual English. In such a case, the English phrase " Even though it should rain cats and dogs¡" hould be used.

212   PROF. ELLIOTT'S LECTURES.

It is well to take as topics for free conversation those that are simple, preferably events of current interest, of which the people generally are talking. A very good side help is the reading of colloquial books—colloquial, it should be observed, not dialectic. Japanese students need not waste time on dialectic English. The teacher's judgment is required in selecting suitable books. "The teacher's judgment, I say," he said. "How evident it becomes, as we look carefully into these questions, that the teacher must never be simply the educated man, the official, but always the personally interested friend and guide of his students!"

His last word on conversation was *practise*. The student who would converse well should practise reading aloud passages which he has already gone over with his teacher, especially colloquial readings. He should practise speaking; if possible, with educated foreigners; with his well-trained teacher, or teachers; with his fellow-students. In the last case, however, he should use only those exercises or selections which he has gone over with his teacher, and in which his mistakes have been indicated; thus practising, not his own errors, but the correct, ordinary, idiomatic English he has learned.

The professor then proceeded to the method of giving lessons in Composition. In composition, as distinct from grammar, students must know the exact meanings of the terms *word, phrase* (particularly reading phrases), *clause, sentence, expression, paragraph, chapter, book, essay, newspaper article*, etc. Before specific study is made in composition, students

PROF. ELLIOTT'S LECTURES. 213

have already acquired some idea of these terms, but in this branch of language study they must be given an accurate conception of them. The teacher must give it to them : by a careful analysis of what each term stands for ; by showing the relations of each to each ; by using many and varied examples.

Punctuation too needs careful analysis and study by the teacher. The best books he had seen were Meiklejohn's "The Art of Writing English," and "English Composition," by Dixon, formerly a professor in the Imperial University ; but he had not seen one that was fully satisfactory. The fact is that scarcely any two English writers agree on this subject, either in theory or practice. So far the learning of punctuation has been left almost entirely to practice and experience.

Some of the best scholars, who read much but write little, are very poor in punctuation ; while others—printers and publishers, for example—though inferior in scholarship, yet, on account of constant practice, punctuate very well indeed. The fact, then, is that, though some valuable rules and suggestions may certainly be given, practice is still the best method in punctuation ; experience the best teacher in it.

Students who are already well drilled in idioms, phrasing, paraphrasing, variation, and such like may now begin to write—not compositions, but composition. One good method is to give them portions of phrases or sentences—catch words—and have them fill these out. Another good one for these beginners is the combining of short sentences into longer ones. A successful plan, here, is to send a number of students—

214   PROF. ELLIOTT'S LECTURES.

say, four—to the board, give them all the same short
sentences, and have each combine them into a long
sentence. Very likely they will combine them in two
or more different ways, all correct or nearly correct.
This diversity is a good thing, and makes it an
exercise both in variation and sentence-building.

Generally speaking, the blackboard should be lib-
erally used in composition as well as in dictation, and
in any branch of language study which aids the student in composing. In this way the eye is impressed
as well as the ear, ;the sound and the form are
directly associated, the mind reached through two
avenues and not one only ; making the impression
nearly, if not quite, doubly strong—as Dr. Stall very
graphically says, "Through eye-gate and ear-gate
into the city of the soul.

The above exercises may be varied with special
drill in the use of *Prepositions* and in the simpler
and more common *Figures of Speech*, particularly
Simile, Metaphor and *Personification*.

Then begin writing *compositions* (not simply learning composition). But let the subjects be very easy
ones at first ; the sentences short ; and simplicity
enjoined. By simplicity he did not mean absence of
idiom, but simple words, and no attempt at the expression of profound or philosophical thought. Let
advancement to this kind of composition be very
gradual, and let the student know that it is necessary
to practise the grace of patience. He may be able
to write pretty well on higher themes in Japanese,
but must not expect it yet in English.

Then the professor ｌspoke of the correction of

PROF. ELLIOTT'S LECTURES. 215

Compositions. It is not well for teachers to do it directly and fully, but rather to *indicate* by a system of suggestive marking. When correcting *is* done, it is well to use the blackboard, and make the corrections there, calling the students' attention to how particular mistakes were made, especially those that arose from carelessness. In case the corrections are made in their composition books, it is necessary to give reasons in all cases where they are not likely to be evident, by footnotes or in some other way.

Mr. Elliott gave a specimen of his system of marking, for illustration. It was as follows :

" The first war with Russia had took place in Chemulpo and second in port arthar early in Feb. | in this year | in both our | warships showed their prowess | and (they) got great victory."

[——Indicates a mistake, or omission ; - a mistake in spelling, punctuation, etc.

| | A word or phrase within these should be replaced by a better one.

(   ) A word or phrase within these had better be omitted.]

The above corrected is :

THE OUTBREAK OF THE WAR.

" The first battle with Russia took place off Chemulpo, and the second off Port Authur, early in February last. In both our navy displayed unusual courage and skill, and won great victories."

216   PROF. ELLIOTT'S LECTURES.

REASONS.

1—The original composition had no title.

2—The abbreviated form is used only in giving *exact* dates.

3—"Prowess" cannot be predicated of inanimate things—only of animals ; chiefly of men.

4—Even in speaking of the navy the more simple and common word is better than "prowess."

CHAPTER IX.

SOME DISTINCTIONS IN ENGLISH.

About thirty Fifth Year class boys, belonging to the First and Second Middle Schools in Kanazawa, were introduced into the lecture-hall; the teacher-students were to observe the way of giving lessons to the boys by the professor. Mr. Elliott spoke of the value of defining synonymous words, remarking that acquaintance with their exact use goes a long way in speaking and writing the language. The lesson he was to give was on distinctions in nouns of similar signification.

First, he asked a question of the boys as to the distinction between grammar and composition. None could give an answer. Hereupon, he simplified his question and asked, "What is grammar?" Still there was none who ventured to stand up and give an answer. The professor then explained the word, and wrote on the blackboard as follows:

"*Grammar* is the art or science of writing or speaking a language correctly, i, e, according to certain rules or principles which determine the forms and constructive relations of words and phrases."

He reminded the audience that the best writers and speakers are not much governed by rules, but that, on the contrary, what they write and speak often determine the rules. After he had tried in vain to make the boys answer his question, "What is

218   PROF. ELLIOTT'S LECTURES.

composition?" he again gave the difinition of it on the blackboard, as:

"*Composition* is the art of writing a language expressively, that is with accuracy, simplicity, clearness and force, and in a way that shows an understanding of the mental and emotional values and effects of words, phrases and longer forms."

He explained in brief the four cardinal points of composition above mentioned. He emphatically urged the importance of using simple words and expressions, claiming that the best writers and speakers generally use simple forms (of expression). The best sermons he had heard were invariably made in simple and clear English. He also advised us to avoid using too much what is called flowery speech, though it is quite proper in its right place and degree. The following distinctions in English were likewise written on the board, and explained by himself:

Color and *Shade*—

"*Color* is more comprehensive; used to denote what is primary or simple."

"*Shade* is used in making fine distinctions, as: A light-red shade; an orange-blown shade. A great variety of shades may be produced by mixing the primary colors."

Promise and *Contract* (or *bargain*)—

"*Promise* strictly and generally is one-sided, an assurance given by one person or set of persons to another or to others. The reference is only to the promising side, and there is no condition, no corresponding promise, from the other side."

"*Contract* (or bargain—a small contract) is two-

PROF. ELLIOTT'S LECTURES. 219

sided, and one man (or set of men) agrees to do something for another (or others) on condition that he (or
they) gets something equivalent in return."

Some more distinctions in English were given during
another hour, but since the lessons were given as he
said, from some papers he had sent to the "Student,"
I omit the mention of them here.

CHAPTER X.

PRACTICAL LESSONS IN READING.

The professor proceeded to show the teacher-students the application of his theory of Oral Reading, by giving practical lessons in reading to the boy-students. He referred to two methods of teaching reading, of which he would speak more particularly in his lectures on "Method in the Study of English" (which see); in one of which the teacher reads first, and is imitated by the students in emphasis, accent, intonation, &.; and in the other the students read first, and are afterwards criticized and set right by the class and the teacher. He would adopt the first of these methods, and have the boys repeat what he read. The readings were taken from "Aesop's Fables." The first lesson was as follows:

THE LION AND THE MOUSE.

A Lion was awakened from *sleep* by a Mouse running over his *face*. Rising up in *anger*, he *caught* him(a) and was about to **kill** him,(b) when the Mouse piteously *entreated*, saying "If you would only *spare* my life, I would be sure to *repay* your kindness." The Lion *laughed* and **let** him **go**. It happened shortly *after* this that the *Lion* was caught by some *hunters*, who bound him by strong ropes to the *ground*.

(The words in Italics are the most emphatic.)

The professor gave several suggestions on Inflection, Emphasis, and Pause, amongst which he remarked :—

PROF. ELLIOTT'S LECTURES. 221

1. The voice falls at (b), because it marks quite a break in the sense at the end of an independent, clause; but the falling inflection at (a) must be very slight, if made at all, because, though the end of an independent clause, the break in the sense is very small.

2. The last word or expression of a series in the same order or construction is more emphatic than those before it, as: "*caught* him," "**kill** him;" "*laughed*," "**let go.**"

3. The word particularized is emphatic.

In the second lesson in reading the some method was followed as on the preceding day.

"Roll on', | thou deep' | and dark' | blue | O' | cean, roll' ! |
Ten thou' | sand fleets' | sweep o' | ver thee' | in vain.' |
Man marks the earth with ruin. His control
Stops with shore. Upon the watery plain
The wrecks are all thy deed."

The foregoing lines were written on the board by the lecturer, who said he had been again asked by some one to explain how to read poems. To read poems according to the feet and accent which they have, as marked in the first two lines, was something never practised by good English readers. He would assure the class again that poem-reading was exactly the same as prose reading, the point being to express naturally the thought and sentiment intended by the

222   PROF. ELLIOTT'S LECTURES.

writer. Care must be taken to avoid "scanning" and a "sing-song style" of reading, which, however, was more common in English-speaking countries than among Japanese students.

The third lesson was given in the same way as previous ones. The theory of "oral reading" was practically applied, several useful suggestions being made in connection with pronunciation.

The fourth and fifth lessons were also given in the same way as on preceding days. Among the suggestions made, the following one way be mentioned:

Transitive verbs in the active voice should be treated as incomplete verbs in reading. and their objects, as complements, be duly emphasized as if the second part of compound verbs, as:

"I am afraid you will fall and break your *neck*."

Let me not forget to state here that Mr. Elliott recited a poem, called "The Red Jacket," in an admirable manner, on the last day of his lectures (Aug. 4th), and that Mr. Ibaraki, of the Kanazawa Higher School, delivered a useful lecture on the methods of teaching foreign languages which now prevail in Germany. I think it a pity that I cannot give here even a gist of his lecture, for want of space.

The Summer School broke up on the 13th. of August. An address was made by Mr. Yoshimura, who was followed by Mr. E. Ando, and Messrs. Mckenzie and Gauntlett. The term of the school was in reality short; nevertheless, the valuable instruction and practical suggestions given by the three experienced professors were greatly appreciated by the earnest company of teachers constituting the class. In conclusion, we have to express our hearty thanks to Messrs. Yoshimura, Hisata, Ando, and Yamamoto, who did all in their power to provide for us every possible convenience while the school lasted.

[THE END.]

不許複製

發行所

東京市神田區裏神保町一番地

三省堂書店

印刷所

東京市神田區三崎河岸第十二號地

三省堂印刷部

發行兼印刷者

東京市神田區裏神保町一番地

龜井忠一

著者

長野縣小縣郡上田町鷹匠町

安藤貫一

明治三十七年十一月廿四日發行

明治三十七年十一月二十日印刷

金澤講習筆記

定價金五十錢

解　題

江利川 春雄
（和歌山大学教育学部教授・日本英語教育史学会会長）

解題

英語教授法研究と教員講習会

　明治後半（1890年代以降）になると、西洋の先進的な学問を英語で学ぶ「英学」の時代は終わり、英語を学校の教科目のひとつとして教授する「英語教育」の時代に移行した。

　中学校の数は1893（明治26）年に全国で74校、進学率はわずか2.1％にすぎなかったが、10年後の1903（明治36）年には269校、進学率6.8％と3倍以上に増加した。さらに高等女学校や実業学校などの中等教育機関も急増した。

　中等教育が普及するにつれて英語の学習者が多様化し、英語力の低下が指摘されるようになる。そのため、教授法の改善が必要になった。また、この時期にはヨーロッパにおける外国語教授法改革も本格化した。こうして、日本においても英語教授法に関する調査・研究が進められるようになった。

　明治期に刊行された主要な外国語教授法書としては以下のものがある（固有名詞以外の旧漢字は新漢字に改めてある。以下同様）。今回復刻した2著はゴチック体で示している。

1887（明治20）年　マーセル著・吉田直太郎訳『外国語研究法』吉田氏蔵版
　　　　　　　　　　　（本シリーズ第2巻で復刻）

1891（明治24）年　磯辺彌一郎編『外国語研究要論』国民英学会

1893（明治26）年　崎山元吉『外国語教授法改良説』崎山元吉

1894（明治27）年　岡倉由三郎『外国語教授新論：附 国語漢文の教授要項』岡
　　　　　　　　　　倉由三郎

1896（明治29）年　松島　剛『英語教授法管見』水野書店
　　　　　　　　　　重野健造『英語教授法改良案』文昌堂

1897（明治30）年　外山正一『英語教授法』大日本図書

1899（明治32）年　内村鑑三『外国語之研究』東京独立雑誌社

1901（明治34）年　八杉貞利『外国語教授法』宝永館書店

1902（明治35）年　佐藤顕理『英語研究法』文聲社

I

ハワード・スワン講述『スワン氏英語教授法』国民英学会出版局

1903（明治36）年　高橋五郎『最新英語教習法』東文館

1904（明治37）年　ガントレットほか講述『明治三十七年夏期金沢英語講習会筆記』三省堂

1906（明治39）年　ブレブナ著・岡倉由三郎訳『外国語最新教授法』大日本図書

1911（明治44）年　岡倉由三郎『英語教育』博文館

　しかし、これまでの英語教授法史研究においては、今回復刻した2つの英語講習会筆記録が本格的に取り上げられることはほとんどなかった。わずかに松村幹男の口頭発表（1980）などがあるのみである。とりわけ『スワン氏英語教授法』（1902）は、現在1冊しか所在が確認できないことからもわかるように、ほとんど研究されてこなかったようである。

文部省主催の中等教員講習会

　文部省は教員の力量向上のために、まず小学校教員を養成する各府県の尋常師範学校教員を対象とする講習会（最初は手工科）を1888（明治21）年から開始した。その後、対象を中学校、高等女学校、実業学校の教員に拡げた。

　教員講習会の目的と意義に関して、文部省は次のように述べている（『日本帝国文部省第三十七年報』1909［明治42］年度、7ページ）。

　教員の学識の多少と教授の巧拙とは教育の進歩発展上至大の関係を有するものなるにより文部省に於ては従来教員の学力を補充し教授法の改善を図るの目的を以て毎年適切なる学科を選定し適当の季節と場所とに於て師範学校、中学校、高等女学校及実業学校等の教員講習会を開設し来りしが近年益々其の効果の顕著なるものあるを認むるに至れり

このように、講習会の目的は「教員の学力を補充し教授法の改善を図る」ことで、講習員（受講者）には修了後に講習員証明書（受講証明書）が交付され、名前と所属が『官報』に告示される場合もあった。文部省主催の講習会は、「英語教員のレベルアップ策としてのみならず、教育政策の中央集権化の一環として位置づけられる」（竹中1995、174ページ）と言えよう。

中等英語科教員に対する文部省主催の第1回の講習会は、1896（明治29）年7月23から8月20日までの4週間、東京の高等師範学校（現・筑波大学）で開催された。同校教授の矢田部良吉が英語教授法について講習し、朗読指導や英訳の課題も出された。各府県から1名程度が選抜されて受講し、33名の講習員中、31名が講習員証明書を受領した。

松村（2011）の調査によれば、文部省主催の英語講習会は1943（昭和18）年までの48年間に、判明しているだけで53回開催された（同一年度の複数開催は個別に数え、文部省後援を一部含む）。

それら英語教員講習会には一流の講師陣が登壇したこともあり、本巻で復刻した2篇以外にも、講習での講義に基づく次のような書籍が出版されている。

・栗原基『英語発達史』博文館、1910年　＊1906（明治39）年の文部省講習会での講義に基づく。
・金子健二『英語基礎学』興文社、1918年　＊1917（大正6）年の文部省講習会での英語史に関する講義に基づく。
・ウィリアム・スイート、飯島東太郎『英国風物談（正・続）』大日本図書、1918年・1921年　＊1916（大正5）年の文部省講習会でのスイートの講義に基づき飯島が編訳。

教授法改革および教員講習会に関しては、帝国教育会もその中心となった。1896（明治29）年に設立された帝国教育会は、小学校から大学までの教員と教

育行政関係者を構成員とする全国規模の組織で、「文部省当局との親和的・翼賛的性格、地方教育会に対する事実上の教育情報発信源としての性格、そして、明治30年代から強められる教育改革的性格を帯びていた」(西原2010、37ページ)。この他にも、民間の国民英学会や正則英語学校(現・正則学園高等学校)、1920年代以降は英語教授研究所(現・語学教育研究所)なども様々な英語教員講習会を開催した。

明治35年文部省英語講習会(東京)でのハワード・スワンの講演

『スワン氏英語教授法』は奥付の表記で、扉のタイトルは The Psychological Method of Teaching and Studying English. By Professor Howard Swan. Arranged by K. Andō. である。1902(明治35)年10月23日、国民英学会出版局(代表・磯辺彌一郎)発行とある。

本書は、1902(明治35)年に東京高等商業学校(現・一橋大学)で開催された文部省夏期英語講習会におけるハワード・スワンの講義内容を、安藤貫一(後述)が英文でまとめたもので、奥付では2人の共著となっている。

なお、『英語教育史資料5』(1980)の「安藤貫一」(8ページ)には、本書が「1903年に国民英学会が Howard Swan を呼んでグアン氏教授法の夏期講習会を開いたときの筆記」と誤記されている。確かにスワンは1903(明治36)年に国民英学会で連続講義をしているが(後述)、本書の刊行は前年の1902(明治35)年であり、本篇の冒頭にも東京高等商業学校での講習であることが明記されている。

この講習会は同年7月25日から8月14日まで3週間にわたって開催され、全国から参集した講習員(受講者)は111名、受講修了証明書である「講習員証明書」

ハワード・スワン(『中外英字新聞』より)

を授与された者は106名だった。

　講師のハワード・スワンはロンドンで生まれ、師と仰ぐフランス人のフランソワ・グアン（François Gouin, 1831～1896）の教授法で指導する外国語学校を経営していた。グアンの教授法書をVictor Bétisと英訳し、*The Art of Teaching and Studying Languages* として1892（明治25）年に刊行した。そのスワンに、渡欧中（1901～1902）の神田乃武（東京高等商業学校教授）が出会い、英語教師として日本に招聘した。そのためスワンは1901（明治34）年9月から1903（明治36）年8月まで、東京高等商業学校で徹底したグアン・メソッドによる英語授業を行った（山川1986、1,065～1,066ページ）。スワンは来日中、次のような著作を刊行している。

The Flashes from the Far East. 博文館、1902年（夏期講習会のテキスト）

Japanese Scenes in English. 博文館、1902年（松田一橘との共著）

English Scenes and Conversations : Lessons on the Psychological Method for Use in Schools. 博文館、1902年

『応用英和新辞典』ABC出版社、1903年（勝俣銓吉郎との共著）

　スワンは講習会で、グアンのPsychological Method（グアン式教授法）に関する17回（原則として各回3時間ずつ）の講話と授業実演を行った。1902（明治35）年8月30日発行の『中外英字新聞』第9巻14号は「文部省英語夏期講習会」と題した記事で次のように報じている（194ページ）。

　文部省の英語夏期講習会は有名なるスワン教授の担当にて其得意の英語教授法を講演することなれば、開会前より一般英学者の視線を惹き、講習員の多き無慮一百十名に及び講師の熱心なる其講演の斬新なる蓋し夏期講習会として空前の成功を収めたるが如し

講習会の内容をまとめた安藤貫一は受講者の一人で、岩手県一関中学校（現・岩手県立一関第一高等学校）の教諭だった。前掲の『中外英字新聞』は「安藤氏の此英文筆記録は講述者〔スワン〕の丁寧なる校閲と増補を加へ種々斬新なる絵画や表をも挿入したれば、之を一読せば親しくスワン氏の講演を聴くが如き利益あらむと信ず」と述べている。ただし、講義をそのまま筆記したものではなく、かなり要約されている。

安藤がまとめた『スワン氏英語教授法』によれば、講習の内容は以下の通りだった。

第1講

　1時間目　Introductory

　2時間目　Sequences of Actions.　Lesson 1　I Open the Door

　3時間目　Reading（テキスト Scott の *Ivanhoe*）

第2講

　1時間目　The Method of Teaching Language

　2時間目　Sequences of Actions.　Lesson 2　I Go Home

　3時間目　Reading（テキスト Scott の *Ivanhoe*）

第3講

　1時間目　On the Teaching of Languages

　2時間目　Sequences of Actions.　Lesson 3　I Go to England

　3時間目　Reading（テキスト Scott の *Ivanhoe*）

第4講

　1時間目　On the Teaching of English

　2時間目　Pronunciation of Well Known Rhymes

　3時間目　Sequences of Actions.　Lesson 4　I Go to England（*Continued*）

第5講

　1時間目　On the Teaching of English

2時間目　Sequences of Actions.　Lesson 5　Waking Up and Breakfasting

3時間目　Reading（テキスト Scott の *Ivanhoe*）

第6講

1時間目　On the Teaching of English

2時間目　Practice Lesson.　Sequences of Actions.　Lesson 6　Washing Hands

3時間目　Cricket ゲームに関する脱線的な講話

第7講

1時間目　On Phonetics

2時間目　Sequences of Actions.　Lesson 7　Breakfast

＊この日はここで授業が終わり、参加者らが九段のレストランでスワン夫妻らを交えて夕食会を開催。

第8講

1時間目　On Prepositions and Subjective Language

2時間目　Sequences of Actions.　Lesson 8　English Student's Life

3時間目　Reading（ここからテキストはスワン著 *Flashes from the Far East*）

第9講

1時間目　On the Subjective Language

2時間目　Sequences of Actions.　Lesson 9　Lighting a Fire

3時間目　Reading（テキストはスワン著 *Flashes from the Far East*）

第10講

1時間目　On the Teaching of Grammar

2時間目　講義はなく写真撮影

3時間目　Reading（テキストはスワン著 *The Flashes from the Far East*）

第11講

1時間目　On Teaching the English Alphabet and the English Language to Beginners

2時間目　Specimen Lesson to Absolute Beginners

3時間目　英語の歌をスワンが歌い解説

第12講

　1時間目　On Grammar (Simple Tenses of Verbs)

　2時間目　Sequences of Actions.　Lesson 10　A Practical Lesson by One of the Students

　3時間目　Reading（テキストはスワン著 *The Flashes from the Far East*）

第13講

　1時間目　On the Teaching of Grammar (Principles and Practice)

　2時間目　Sequences of Actions.　Lesson 11　Going Out in a Car

　3時間目　Reading（テキストはスワン著 *Flashes from the Far East*）

第14講

　1時間目　On Colloquial and Literary English

　2時間目　受講者による模擬授業とスワンの講評

　3時間目　Reading（テキストはスワン著 *The Flashes from the Far East*）

第15講

　1時間目　On the Teaching of Literature

　2時間目　Sequences of Actions.　Lesson 12　Calling on a Friend and Lesson 13　The Visit

　3時間目　なし

第16講

　1時間目　Summary

　2時間目　Sequences of Actions.　Lesson 14　Rowing

　3時間目　Reading（テキストはスワン著 *The Flashes from the Far East*）

第17講（最終）

　1時間目　Summary

　2時間目　Sequences of Actions.　Lesson 15　Objective and Subjective

　3時間目　Reading（テキストはスワン著 *The Flashes from the Far East*）

以上のように、1時間目には英語教授法、音声・発音指導、文字指導、文法指導、口語と文語、文学指導法などについての多彩な講義を行い、2時間目にはグアン式教授法の最大の特徴である Sequences of Actions（時間的に連続する一連の動作）をほぼ毎回にわたって実地指導している。その上で、3時間目に仕上げとしてリーディング指導を行っていたことがわかる。

　ただし、ときにはクリケットの話で脱線し、受講者の要望に応えて英語の歌を歌い、講義を早めに切り上げて受講者と夕食会を催すなど、ほほえましい光景も見られた。他方、第11講の終了後には、スワン提唱の教授法を日本の中等教育でどう実施するかについての真剣な討論会も行われている。

　なお、この講習会の概要については、S. ISHII が「スワン氏英語教授法」として『中外英字新聞』第9巻第14号（1902年8月30日）198ページに英文で記している。

　スワンは翌1903（明治36）年7月27日から8月8日まで、文部省に代わって国民英学会が主催した中等学校英語教員夏期講習会でもグアン式教授法を講じた。中学校、師範学校の教員を中心に全国から36名が参集し、毎日平均4時間の講習を受け、スワン宅での茶話会なども催された（『中外英字新聞』第10巻第14号、193ページ。同誌第10巻第10号と12号にも関連記事）。

　講習直後の8月22日、スワンは清国（中国）の学校に赴任するために離日した。英語教育史研究者の大村喜吉は、「Swan の滞在はわずか3年（1901～03）にすぎなかったが、その来日とそのグアン＝メソッドはそれなりの貢献と影響を日本の英学界に残していったと見てよい」（大村1980、128ページ）と評価している。

グアン式教授法とその影響

　グアンの言語教授法は、ドイツ語習得に失敗した自らの経験を省察することによって考案された。外国語の習得においても幼児が母語を習得するのと同様に、思考の順序に従った自然な流れで教材を配置し、時間的に連続する一連

9

の動作（Sequences of Actions）に従いながら言語を理解させる。口と耳による音声言語の習得と反復を重視し、母語への翻訳は行わない。そのためグアンの教授法はSeries Method（連続法）、Natural Method（自然教授法）、Psychological Method（心理学的教授法）とも呼ばれる。

　グアンの教授法は、スワンによる講習に続いて、1904（明治37）年の金沢における文部省夏期英語講習会においても講師のマッケンジーが7回にわたって講義するなど（後述）、日本の英語教育界への影響を見過ごすことはできないようである。

　これらを踏まえて、片山寛（東京外国語学校〔現・東京外語大学〕教授）は『我国に於ける英語教授法の沿革』（1935）で、「規則や術語の暗記等 grammar 一点張の英学界に Swan 氏の投じた一石は其当時多大の反響を起こした」（24ページ）と評価している。

　それでは、明治期日本の英語教育界は、グアンの教授法をどのように受容し評価していたのだろうか。代表的な見解を見てみたい。

　愛媛県師範学校教諭だった杢田與惣之助（1882〜1960　＊詳細は本シリーズ第3巻「解題」参照）は、授業用のプリント『英語教授法綱要』（1909）の「欧米に於ける近世外国語教授の諸方法」で代表的な9つの教授法を紹介しており、「グアン法」についても次のように詳細に紹介している。

　　第五、グアン法
　　此法は仏人グアン氏の創始せるものにして、氏は一八八〇年に其著 *The Art of Teaching and Studying Languages*〔原典はフランス語版〕を公にしたり、此法は或外国語中の最も普通なる語を簡単なる文章の形に於て彙類〔＝分類〕し、こを或る群に分ち、各群の語を共通の主格に結合せしむ、而して一群が一課をなし各課集りて一節をなし、数節相合して一章を作る、かくの如く一の series をなすを以て此を The Series Method と称す、蓋し観念連合及心的現像の原理の上に立ちたるものにして、今日に於ても尚多く用ゐられつゝ

あるものなり、今此方法の実際を見るに、教師は各課を先づ口頭にて授け次に書につきて読ましめ又は板書して読ましむ、新語を教授するや教師は生徒をして眼を閉ぢて其の語の内容につきての心像を喚起せしめ以て幾多の語句の連結を鞏固（きょうこ）にし以て一か喚起せらるゝときは直に他が連絡して生起する様ならしむるものなり、然れども此法にも実物絵画を使用する□□□□〔4字判読不能〕にあらず、教授中には自国語を用ゐるを妨げず、話は多く教師之を行ひ、生徒は不断に之を繰返し又教師の問に答ふ、而して一課を終れば□〔1字判読不能〕に作文の教授を行ひ、文法教授の如きも早くより之を行ふ、然れども爾余の練習と結合せんことを力（つと）む、連続的の文章に至ては之を単語集の終れる後に行ふ。

（一）此法の利
　　動詞に重（おもき）を置き文法上の仕組に巧なること
　　心理的原理に立てること
（二）此法の不利
　　組織の精密に過ぎ活用の途乏しきこと
　　連環語中の或物は教授に不適当なること
　　全く想像によらんとし実物絵画等を棄てたること

このように、杢田はグアン式教授法の長所と短所を冷静に分析している。
　次に、英語教育界の代表格だった岡倉由三郎は、『教育大辞書』（同文館、1907）所収の「英語教授法（小学校における）」（122〜126ページ）で、「初期の語学教授に最適な方法」として、グアンのNatural Methodを推奨している（ただし代筆の可能性がある）。

種々の点より考ふるに、畢竟自然的方法（Natural Method）に依るを以て最も可なりとすべし。即ち生徒の年齢や四辺の状態を斟酌して生徒が自国語を

学ぶと同様に感ぜしむる様にして英語の基本的観念を教へ込むにあり。此際文字は無論教ふることなく日本語も是非必要を覚ゆる場合の外は決して用ふることなし、実物又は実地の動作を示して、直ちにこれを英語にて発表することを教ふるなり。

　安部磯雄（早稲田大学教授）の考えも岡倉に近い。本復刻シリーズの第7巻に収めた『英語研究苦心談』（97〜120ページ）での講演「グーアンの外国語習得法」で、安部は、「グーアンの所謂子供すらも六ヶ月で〔外〕国語を覚えるのだから、吾々が六ヶ月でもってどんな国語でも覚えられない筈はない。これはグーアンの原則で私は今でもさういふ確信をもって居ります」（117ページ）と述べている。
　こうした賛成論の一方で、英学者の高橋五郎は1903（明治36）年に刊行した『最新英語教習法』（190ページ）で、グアンの教授法とそれを推奨するハワード・スワンを強烈に批判した。

　自然式または直接式なる者は、嬰児教育法を取て直ちに少年教育法に転用し、母語教習法を以て直ちに外国語教育法と為したる背心理的教習法にして、取るに足らず、グアン式は愚案式なりとは我を欺かざる哉、スワン氏の如きが今尚該式を我国に振まはしつゝあるは寧ろ奇とすべし（圏点と下線は高橋）

　では、直接スワンから講習を受けた人たちへの影響はどうだったのだろうか。受講時に中学校教諭で、のちに同志社大学教授となった南石福二郎（1883〜1972）は次のように述べている（『英語新教授法の実際』はしがき）。

　顧みれば著者は二十五年前英語に於けるBaphometic BaptismをHoward Swan氏に受け、爾来十数年中学校に於ける英語教育に従事して居た間に幾分之

を実験し、新教授法の価値を慥(たしか)めて来た

　このように、スワンが播いた種は南石のような日本人教師に引き継がれ、一部の学校現場で実践されていったのである。

　グアンの言語教授法は、英語教授法のみならず、日本語教授法（例えば山口喜一郎の直接教授法）にも大きな影響を与えた。日本統治時代の台湾では、公学校における第二言語としての日本語教授法の参考資料として、グアンの *The Art of Teaching and Studying Languages*（前述）を台湾総督府国語学校教授の橋本武が抄訳し、『ゴアン氏言語教授方案』として 1900（明治33）年7月に刊行した。これは 1902（明治35）年夏の文部省英語講習会におけるハワード・スワンの講演の2年前である。

　台湾総督府民政部学務課は、同書を刊行した理由を「緒言」で次のように述べている。

　ゴアン氏の言語教授法は、之を国語学校第一附属学校に於て、国語科の教授に実験したるに、其の成蹟甚だ見るべきものあり。因て今回学務課に於て編纂したる会話書及び公学読本の如きも、主として此法に基きたり。故に本島公学校に於ける国語教授の参考に供せんが為めに、此書を印刷に附せり。

　このように、日本においては英語教育よりも以前に、植民地台湾における日本語教育の進展という帝国主義的な教育政策の一環として、グアンの教授法がいち早く採用されていたのである（王2011）。

明治37年夏期金沢英語講習会

　1904（明治37）年の夏に金沢で開催された文部省英語講習会の内容は、受講者の一人である安藤貫一がまたも筆記・編集し、『明治三十七年夏期金沢

英語講習会筆記』（扉のタイトルは *Résumé of Lectures Given at the Summer School of English* (1904) *by Prof. Gauntlett, Prof. McKenzie, Prof. Elliott, Written and Arranged by K. Ando.*）として、同年11月24日に東京の三省堂から刊行された。3人の外国人講師による講述で、彼らの校閲も経ているが、奥付の著者名は安藤貫一だけとなっている。

この本は講習会の内容をかなり詳細に再現しているため、本編が223ページに及び、2年前に刊行された『スワン氏英語教授法』の本編64ページと比べると3.5倍にもなる。

1904（明治37）年5月20日の『官報』6265号に掲載された「文部省告示第121号」によれば、「師範学校中学校高等女学校教員等夏期講習会」は7月25日から8月14日までの3週間、金沢の第四高等学校（現・金沢大学）で開催された。講師は登壇順に、第六高等学校（現・岡山大学）教師のエドワード・ガントレット（George Edward Luckman Gauntlett, 1868〜1956）、元第四高等学校教師のダニエル・マッケンジー（Daniel Rial McKenzie, 1861〜1935）、広島高等師範学校（現・広島大学）教師のウイリアム・エリオット（William Elliott, 1856〜?）の3人、講習員は各道府県から1〜2名ずつ参集した合計61人だった。

ガントレットは1868年にウェールズに生まれた。ロンドンで音楽や美術などを学び、カナダで宣教師となる。1891（明治24）年に来日し、東京の高等商業学校、千葉中学校、麻布中学校で英語を教えたのち、1899（明治32）年に第六高等学校に6年間在職。金沢の第四高等学校を経て、1907（明治40）年に山口高等商業学校（現・山口大学）で8年半教え、1919（大正8）年には東京の立教大学嘱託講師として1936（昭和11）年まで在職、1941（昭和16）年に日本に帰化した。ガントレットは商業英語、速記、英習字などの実用英語の教授法を日本に導入し、エスペラント語の普及にも尽力した（武内1995、92〜93ページ）。

マッケンジーは1861年にエリオットと同じカナダ・オンタリオ州に生まれ、ヴィクトリア大学を卒業。その後ウエスレアン神学校で神学博士号を取得し、宣教師として1888（明治21）年に来日、金沢の第四高等学校で英語教師となっ

た。1892（明治25）年からは北陸での伝道に従事し、日露戦争中は赤十字とともに傷病兵の慰問や出征兵士の留守家族救援のために奔走、金沢に育児院を設立した。1910（明治43）年に関西学院の理事に就任、特に高等商業学部の充実・発展に尽くし、1933（昭和8）年の定年まで務めた（関西学院大学2014）。

エリオットは1856年にカナダのオンタリオ州に生まれ、1884年にヴィクトリア大学を卒業。宣教師として来日し、創立直後の広島高等師範学校で、1902（明治35）年10月から1909（明治42）年7月まで7年近く英語を教えた。エリオットの講義に関して、1909（明治42）年に同校予科に入学した上田畊甫は「先生は文部省中等教員講習のテキスト Oral Reading という本で、朗読法を錬磨された」と述べている（松村1978、52ページ）。エリオットは、金沢での講習会でも Oral Reading を5回にわたって行っている（後述）。

では、彼らの金沢での講習会はいかなる内容だったのだろうか。講習回数は、ガントレットが20回（10〜105ページ）、マッケンジーが13回（106〜182ページ）、エリオットが10回（183〜223ページ）で、冒頭の挨拶も含めれば合計44回の講習だったことがわかる。

『明治三十七年夏期金沢英語講習会筆記』の構成

刊行された『明治三十七年夏期金沢英語講習会筆記』（1904）では、講習の各回を章（Chapter）として順番に配列している（ただし、章番号に脱落があり、その箇所は注記した）。そのため、以下に示した同書の構成と内容を見れば、講習の全体像がわかる。

序文
開会の挨拶（第四高等学校校長・吉村寅太郎）
第1章　マッケンジーによる開講の挨拶
〈ガントレットによる講習　20回〉
第2〜6章　Phonetics

第7～9章　Writing and Penmanship

第10章　Preposition

第11章　Corrections

第12章　Clauses and Phrases　（＊第13章は原本にない）

第14章　Fluency in Speaking English

第15～21章　Conversation

＜マッケンジーによる講習　13回＞

第1章　The Gouin System

第2～7章　Natural Method

第8・14章　A Study in the English Poets　（＊9～13章は原本にない）

第15章　English Prose Writers

第16章　The Subjunctive Mood

第17章　"Shall" and "Will"

第18章　The Relatives "that" and "which"

＜エリオットによる講習　10回＞

第1章　Introductory to Oral Reading

第2～5章　Oral Reading

第6～8章　Method in the Study of English

第9章　Some Distinctions in English

第10章　Practical Lessons in Reading

　このように、ガントレットは音声学、文字指導などに続き英会話のレッスンに多くの時間を割いている。マッケンジーは前半でグアンの教授法を講習し、後半では英国の詩人や作家、重要な文法事項を扱っている。エリオットは前半でオーラル・リーディングを、後半で英語の研究法やリーディング演習を行っている。なお、講習会では中学生を相手に授業実演も行った。

　前述の『官報』6265号には講師ごとの「英語講習要目」が事前に掲載され

ていたが、実際の講習内容は予告とはかなり異なっている。たとえば、講習の最後の方では3人一緒のレッスンを行うと予告されていたが、実際には最後まで単独で行われた。

金沢での講習会に関して、『中外英字新聞』第11巻9号（1904〔明治37〕年9月15日）は「文部省夏期講習会の景況」と題した記事を掲載している。かなり正確な内容である。

　三講師の内最も評判好かりしはガントレット氏であったらしく、同氏は石川県第一及び第二中学校の一年級生徒三十六人に習字のレッスンを与へ同第五年級生徒に会話及び作文を教へて実地教授法を講習員に示めし。マッケンジー氏は同第三年級生徒に得意のNatural Methodを応用して教えたるが同じレッスンを四五日間に亘りて教えたり。又エリオット氏にはOral Readingと云ふ題にて五年級の中学校生徒にreadingを教えたるが其前にemphasisやpauseの説明を与へたり。（中略）ガントレット氏の習字の教え方と英語の発音法は最も講習員に満足を与へたらしく氏の多芸多能なるには一同感服したり。

このように、受講者は3週間にわたる英語漬けの環境で、上記のような盛りだくさんの内容を学び、英語力と英語教授法を磨く実地訓練を積んだ。参加した中等英語教員の実力にも驚かされるが、それ以上に、受講者として講習の内容を的確に筆記・要約した安藤貫一の英語力には驚嘆すべきものがある。では、安藤とはどのような人物だったのだろうか。

安藤貫一（1878〜1925）

　安藤貫一は1878（明治11）年に東京深川に生まれ、ジェームス・サマーズの欧文正鵠学館を経て、磯辺彌一郎の国民英学会英文科を卒業し、1898（明治31）年に三重県立四日市商業学校講師となった。以後、茨城県師範学校、青森

県師範学校で英語を教え、1901（明治34）年には22歳で難関の師範学校中学校高等女学校教員検定試験（英語科）に合格した。その後は教諭として岩手県立一関中学校（講習会参加時）、長野県立上田中学校、鹿児島県立第一中学校、京城（ソウル）の朝鮮総督府中学校で教えた。

この間、1909（明治42）年7月から1911（明治44年）3月まで島津男爵の案内役としてアメリカ・イギリスの旅行に随行し、

安藤貫一（『安藤貫一教授追悼録』より）

英国ではロンドン大学、米国ではロチェスター大学で英文学および英語音声学などを学んだ。

1916（大正5）年に大阪に転居し、大阪貿易学校講師を経て、1918（大正7）年6月に大阪市立高等商業学校（現・大阪市立大学）教授、同校校友会語学部長となった。1924（大正13）年7月には英文学研究のため欧米に留学したが、ボストン大学にて研究中に健康を害し、同年12月にイギリスに渡り、ワイト島にて療養中の翌年1月27日に46歳で逝去した。

1925（大正14）年には長男の安藤誠一の編集で『安藤貫一教授追悼録』が私家版として刊行された。同書は、『英語青年』に掲載された磯辺彌一郎、大谷繞石、岡倉由三郎、勝俣銓吉郎、武信由太郎、細江逸記などの錚々たる英学者の追悼文を中心に編集されたものである。その中で、岡倉由三郎（東京高等師範学校〔現・筑波大学〕教授）は、安藤の英語力を次のように評価している（54ページ）。

自分は、安藤氏をただ能文の気に富んだ学界の強の者として敬服し、氏が英語の雅俗各様の語句をば、さながら、能筆の書家が真字仮字を好んで種々の体に書き却すあの自由さ、あの冴えざえしさに引き比べて、驚嘆の舌を

捲いてゐたのであった。

また、国民英学会の磯辺彌一郎は、ハワード・スワンの夏期講習会を聴講した安藤の筆記の様子を次のように述べている（同書6ページ）。

毎日のレクチュアを一々詳細に筆記し、沢山の図解も洩らす所なく之を写し取り、講習会が終了した時には一個の立派な本が出来た。之を見て私は安藤氏に勧めて印刷に附し、The Psychological Method of Teaching English〔正しくは The Psychological Method of Teaching and Studying English〕と題して出版した。西洋人のレクチュアを此の如く詳細に聴取ることが出来るといふことは大概の日本英学者には一寸出来ない芸当であって、これを見ても安藤氏が手や口ばかりでなく耳までも英語に敏であったことが知れる。

このような卓越した英語力によって、安藤は以下のような日本文学の英訳を刊行している。

・*I Am a Cat.*（夏目漱石『吾輩は猫である』）大倉書店、1909年
・*The Serene Realm beyond the Passion.*（菊池寛『恩讐の彼方に』）研究社、1922年
・*Shunkan.*（倉田百三『俊寛』）研究社、1925年

このほか、1911（明治44）年から翌年にかけて「佐倉宗五郎伝」の英訳"Sakura Sōgorō, Martyr" を『中外英字新聞』に15回連載した。

文部省などが主催した中等英語教員講習会の内容および歴史的意義に関しても、2つの講習内容を筆記・刊行した安藤貫一についても、研究は不十分なままである。今回の復刻が今後の研究の進展に寄与できれば幸いである。

参考文献

安藤誠一編（1925）『安藤貫一教授追悼録』安藤誠一発行

大村喜吉（1980）「スワン」大村ほか編『英語教育史資料5』東京法令出版

岡倉由三郎（1907）「英語教授法（小学校における）」『教育大辞書』同文館

片山寛（1935）『我国に於ける英語教授法の沿革』研究社（英語教育叢書）

関西学院大学（2014）「マッケンジー，D.R.」『関西学院事典 増補改訂版』（電子版）

　　https://www.kwansei.ac.jp/r_history/r_history_008536.html　（2018年10月5日検索）

Gouin, François（1892）*The Art of Teaching and Studying Languages*.（Translated from the French by Howard Swan and Victor Bétis）. G. Philip.（復刻版 Foundations of Foreign Language Teaching, Vol. 6, Routledge, 2000）

ゴアン著・橋本武抄訳（1900）『ゴアン氏言語教授方案』台湾総督府民政部学務課〔*The Art of Teaching and Studying Languages* の抄訳〕

国民英学会出版局編（1903）「（英学時評）スワン氏英語夏期講習会」『中外英字新聞』第10巻第14号（8月30日発行）

国民英学会出版局編（1904）「文部省夏期講習会の景況」『中外英字新聞』第11巻9号（9月15日発行）

高橋五郎（1903）『最新英語教習法』東文館

武内博編著（1995）『来日西洋人名事典　増補改訂版』日外アソシエーツ

竹中龍範（1995）「第1回文部省英語科講習会（明治29年）について」『英語教育研究』第37・38合併号、広島大学英語教育学会

出来成訓（1980）「安藤貫一」大村喜吉ほか編『英語教育史資料5』東京法令出版

出来成訓（1994）『日本英語教育史考』東京法令出版

西原雅博（2010）「帝国教育会英語教授法研究部の成立」『富山高等専門学校紀要』第1号

杰田與惣之助（1909）『英語教授法綱要』私家版（＊本シリーズ第3巻「解題」参照）

松村幹男（1978）「広島高師の外国人教師：Elliott, Smith および Pringle」『英学史研究』第10号

松村幹男（1980）「明治37年金沢英語講習会について」第17回日本英学史学会全国大会（1980年10月25～27日、金沢市）での口頭発表資料

松村幹男（1997）『明治期英語教育研究』辞游社

解 題

松村幹男（2011）「文部省主催中等教員英語講習会：広島開催の事例を中心に」『英學史論叢』
　　　第14号、日本英学史学会中国四国支部
南石福二郎（1926）『英語新教授法の実際』開拓社
文部省（1911）『日本帝国文部省第三十七年報』文部大臣官房文書課
山川喜久男（1986）「英語：一橋英語百年の歩み」一橋大学学園史編集委員会編『一橋大学
　　　学問史：一橋大学創立百年記念』一橋大学
王 秋陽（2011）「日本統治時代の台湾における日本語教育：グアン氏言語教授法に関連して」
　　　『東アジア研究』第9号、山口大学大学院東アジア研究科

英語教育史重要文献集成　第8巻
英語教員講習1

2018年11月26日　初版発行

監修・解題　江利川春雄

発　行　者　荒井秀夫

発　行　所　株式会社 ゆまに書房
　　　　　　東京都千代田区内神田 2-7-6
　　　　　　郵便番号　101-0047
　　　　　　電　　話　03-5296-0491（代表）

印　　　刷　株式会社 平河工業社

製　　　本　東和製本 株式会社

定価：本体 12,000 円＋税

ISBN978-4-8433-5461-2 C3382

落丁・乱丁本はお取替えします。